Vegetarian Delights

Millan Chessman

All rights reserved. Written permission must be secured from the publisher to use or reproduce any part of this book, except for brief quotations in critical reviews or articles.

Printed in the United States of America.

ISBN 0-9776259-0-7

Introduction

In the Bible, Daniel 1:8 states that Daniel was chosen by the king of Babylon to serve in his palace. Daniel was offered the "delicacies" that the king ate. But Daniel insisted on eating the Genesis 1:29 diet of vegetables and water and not to defile his body. Webster's Dictionary defines "defile" to make foul, to make filthy, or dirty, pollute, corrupt, violate. These are strong words, but this is exactly what we do to our bodies when we eat these "delicacies" daily. Look around you. Eighty percent of adult Americans are overweight, and even more heartbreaking is that the children are sick and obese as well.

After 10 days in the Babylonian palace, the result of Daniel's diet showed good health, academic prowess, and a special ability to understand the meaning of dreams and visions. WOW!

God made foods are fruits, vegetables, grains, legumes, raw nuts and raw seeds. Man-made foods (delicacies that defile) are processed foods, enriched white flower, white sugar, animal products and foods with additives and preservatives. The choice is yours.

You will find in the Bible that prior to the flood when man ate only the Genesis 1:29 diet, the life span is recorded as long as 968 years. After the flood man's life span dropped to 100 years when man included animal products in his diet. Prior to the flood there was no sickness or disease recorded.

Thank you for your interest in my cookbook. You will find that the desserts featured are not as sweet as usual recipes.

The cover photo shows me serving my husband. It is said that the way to a man's heart is through his stomach. That's not true, but cute nonetheless. I believe a healthy, loving marriage is the wife serving her husband and the husband serving his wife. A man can't help but be loving and kind when his wife prepares a delicious meal for him. This has been my experience.

Some healthful and helpful hints:

- Read over the recipe first and have all the ingredients handy before you start.
- *Always* use mineral salt.
- Fresh garlic should be added last whenever possible for nutritional benefit and flavor.
- When recipe calls for eggs, most of the time (not all) remove the yolk and use only the egg white. For added moisture, add extra egg white. Also use egg substitute.
- *Always* substitute soy milk for regular milk and soy cream for regular cream. I use all kinds of soy, not only fermented, but be sure it is not genetically engineered. Use organic.
- To cook legumes (bean family): Fill a large jar with water and legumes; soak overnight. The next day, drain water and rinse legumes thoroughly. Place legumes back into jar and lay jar on its side with legumes spread out. Cover opening with cheese cloth (or cut panty hose) and rubber band. Rinse legumes three times a day for three days. Green sprouts will begin to grow. These are very nutritious. Cook covered in pot of water with a vegetable bouillon cube till tender, usually about 30 minutes.
- Use spices like Spike, Dash and Indo in recipes, usually 2 teaspoons will do. They enhance the flavor of food.

Contents

Sauces and Dressings 1-11

Side Dishes 13-21

Soups 23-37

Salads 39-60

Main Dishes 61-157

Desserts 159-180

Biography 181

To my wonderful husband, Jeffrey J. Fout,
for trying out my experimental recipes and
giving me your honest evaluation.

◆

Thank you, world evangelist Bill Rudge
and your lovely wife Karen, for your input and
suggestions in writing this cookbook.
Your healthy lifestyle and knowledge
is greatly appreciated.

◆

To my family and dear friends
for the recipes shared in this cookbook.

◆

To my golden retriever, Chessler,
for eating everything I prepared
that was not acceptable
for this cookbook.

◆

Sweet and Sour Sauce

¼ cup tamari
¼ cup sherry
¼ cup vinegar
1 teaspoon sorghum syrup or barley malt
¼ teaspoon ginger grated
1 teaspoon green onion, chopped
2 teaspoons arrowroot powder
1 teaspoon sesame oil
½ green or red sweet pepper, chopped
½ onion chopped
1 teaspoon sesame seeds
2 cloves garlic, crushed

In a small bowl combine tamari, sherry, vinegar, sorghum, ginger, green onion and garlic. Stir in the arrowroot, making sure there are no lumps. Heat the sesame oil in a frying pan until hot but not smoking. Sauté the onion and pepper until vegetables are soft. Making sure that the arrowroot is still well mixed, pour the tamari mixture onto the vegetables while constantly stirring. Heat until sauce is clear and thickened. Sprinkle sesame seeds on top.

Cucumber Dressing

Blend all:
2 cucumbers, peeled and cut
Juice of 2-3 limes or lemons
½ cup virgin olive oil
4 garlic cloves
Salt to taste

Emergency Dressing

½ cup lemon juice
½ cup virgin olive oil
⅛ cup Bragg's liquid aminos
¼ cup pure water
4 cloves crushed garlic
1 heaping tablespoon Spike

Mix all in blender.

Yogurt Dressing (Arabic)

Blend:
6 tablespoons sesame seeds
1 cup plain soy yogurt
Juice of 2 limes
4 garlic cloves
½ cup virgin olive oil
1 rounded tablespoon Spike
Salt to taste

Millan's Healthy and Delicious Salad Dressing

3 cloves garlic
¼ cup virgin olive oil
¼ cup raw apple cider vinegar
¼ cup raw tahini
1 teaspoon lemon juice
2 teaspoons Spike seasoning
Salt to taste (1 teaspoon or more)
Pepper to taste
2 tablespoons ground flax seed
2 tablespoons Dulse Flakes Sea Vegetables
Water as needed (approximately ¼ cup)

Blend completely in blender.
Refrigerate, will last 7 days.

Eggplant Cream

1 large eggplant (about 2 pounds)
1 tablespoon lemon juice
2 tablespoons virgin olive oil
1 tablespoon Spike
2 cloves garlic finely smashed
Salt and pepper
1-2 tablespoons plain soy yogurt

Bake eggplant in 450 F oven for about 30 minutes until evenly charred and soft all over. Peel off skin and mash pulp. Add lemon juice, oil, Spike, garlic and salt and pepper to taste. Stir in yogurt. Serve as a dip with pita or raw vegetables.

Spicy Sesame Sauce

2 tablespoons sesame butter
2 tablespoons water
1 tablespoon tamari
¼ to ½ teaspoon spicy hot sesame oil (or same amount toasted sesame oil with a dash of cayenne pepper)

In a small bowl, stir together the sesame butter with water until very smooth. Stir in the tamari and the hot sesame oil* until well combined.

*You can also add any or all of the following for a change of flavor: 1 teaspoon crushed sesame seeds, ½ teaspoon vinegar, ½ teaspoon sorghum syrup, ¼ teaspoon grated ginger, ¼ teaspoon minced garlic, 1 tablespoon minced cilantro or parsley.

This sauce is good tossed with cold or hot wheat or rice noodles, raw julienned cucumber, and bean sprouts. This sauce is good on grains, salads and vegetables.

Cream Sauce

¼ cup olive oil
⅓ cup whole wheat flour
3 cloves garlic, minced
1 small onion, finely chopped
1 small carrot, finely chopped
4-5 cups soy milk
Dash of cayenne powder
Big dash of cumin powder
Big dash of paprika
2 teaspoons salt
2-4 tablespoons parsley, minced

Heat the olive oil in a large frying pan until hot but not smoking. Sauté half the onion for about 2 minutes. Quickly stir in the flour all at once making sure there are no lumps. Continue to simmer this mixture, stirring occasionally, until the flour is medium brown. Stir in the other half of the onion, carrot, and garlic. Stir in the soy milk slowly and combine well. Bring back to a simmer. Stir in the cayenne, cumin, paprika, and salt. Sprinkle the parsley on top. This sauce is good on grains, pasta, vegetables. Also good with baked potato. Scoop out potato, mix in sauce and put back into empty skins.

Hummus

(serves 2-3)

---

1 15 ounce can chick peas, drained or cook your own
2 tablespoons tahini, raw
2 tablespoons fresh lemon juice
1 garlic clove, crushed
Salt and ground black pepper to taste
Olive oil and paprika pepper, to garnish

To serve:

Selection of salad vegetables, e.g., cucumber, chicory, baby corn, pepper strips, radishes

Pita bread

Put the chick peas, tahini, lemon juice, garlic and plenty of seasoning into a food processor or blender and mix to a smooth paste.

Spoon the hummus into a bowl and swirl the top with the back of a spoon. Trickle over a little olive oil and sprinkle with paprika. Serve with pita bread or vegetables.

Chip Dip (Guacamole)

4 tomatillos cut in quarters
2 medium tomatoes cut in quarters
3 cloves of garlic
½ onion cut in half
2 avocados
1-2 serrano chilis cut in half—or to taste
1 teaspoon Mexican seasoning
1 rounded teaspoon salt
1 cup finely chopped cilantro

Blend tomatillos, garlic and serrano chilis high until smooth.

Add all other ingredients and blend on chop or low until tiny lumps.

Hummus Trio
(serves 4)

1 16 ounce can garbanzo beans, drained and rinsed or cook your own
Juice of 1 lemon
2 tablespoon fresh minced garlic
1 tablespoon salt
2 ounces olive oil
2 ounces cold water
4 ounces raw tahini
½ cup fresh cilantro leaves
½ cup roasted red peppers

In a food processor or blender, add garbanzo beans, lemon juice, sesame tahini, salt, olive oil, water and garlic and process until smooth. Divide into three portions. Add ⅓ cup roasted red bell peppers to processor or blender and chop; return one portion of blended mixture to processor or blender and process red peppers until smooth. Clean processor or blender. Add cilantro leaves to processor or blender and process remaining hummus mixture with cilantro until smooth. Serve as dips or sandwich spreads.

Italian Salad Dressing

1 cup orange juice
¼ cup lemon juice
2 tablespoons raw apple cider vinegar
1 tablespoon raw agave nectar, or raw sugar
2 medium cloves garlic, pressed or diced
1½ cups olive oil
1 tablespoon Italian seasoning
1 tablespoon dried parsley

Blend in blender until creamy. Delicious! Keeps about 1 week in the refrigerator.

Variation: For complete protein and EFA (essential fatty acids) boost, add 1 tablespoon flax seeds, ground to a fine powder in your coffee grinder. Blend with the other ingredients.

Green Salad Dressing

¾ cup raw apple cider vinegar
1 cup olive oil
¼ cup water
1 rounded teaspoon salt
1 heaping tablespoon Dash
5 cloves of garlic
¼ cup Bragg's liquid aminos
½ raw pumpkin seeds
1 cup fresh parsley, pressed down

Blend all ingredients.

Creamy Corn Salsa

3 ears fresh corn, off the cob, or one can corn
1 red bell pepper, diced
2 medium avocados, chopped
1 yellow summer squash, grated
1 small red onion, diced
2 medium tomatoes, chopped
2 oranges, juiced
1 lime, juiced
1 teaspoon salt
1 clove garlic, pressed
1 small handful parsley
½ cup cilantro, chopped
¼ teaspoon cayenne
2 teaspoon Mexican seasoning

Combine in a medium mixing bowl the first four ingredients and set aside. In a food processor, add remaining ingredients and pulse until well combined. Mixture should be in small pieces and slightly creamy, rather than completely liquefied. Add contents of the food processor to the corn mixture in the bowl, and stir well.

Magic Johnson's Southern-Style Collard Greens

(serves 4)

2 cups water
¼ cup diced onion
1 bay leaf
½ teaspoon allspice
½ teaspoon minced fresh garlic
1 tablespoon Worcestershire sauce (vegetarian if possible)
2 teaspoons tamari
¼ teaspoon cumin
1 teaspoon honey
4 cups chopped fresh collard greens
1 tablespoon olive oil
Salt, black pepper and cayenne pepper to taste

In medium pot, combine water, onion, bay leaf, allspice, garlic, Worcestershire sauce, tamari, cumin and honey. Bring to a boil, reduce heat and simmer for 5 minutes. Add collard greens and return to a boil. Reduce heat and simmer, covered, until greens are tender (about 30 minutes).

Remove pot from heat; cool slightly. Remove bay leaf and stir in oil. Add salt, pepper and cayenne to taste. Serve hot. Oh so good!

Side Dishes

Sugar Snap Pea Sauté with Mushrooms and Corn
(serves 6)

Slicing the sugar snap peas in half into thin "canoes" makes this sauté more elegant than a stir-fry and easier to eat.

2 tablespoons olive oil or butter
1 large leek, cleaned and chopped
¼ pound mushrooms, stems removed and sliced
2 cloves garlic, minced
2 cups sugar snap peas, sliced in half lengthwise
1½ cups corn
½ cup chopped fresh basil
8 ounces fresh, mini-mozzarella balls drained and halved

Heat olive oil in large skillet over medium heat. Sauté leek, mushrooms and garlic 5-6 minutes, or until leek is soft and mushrooms are tender.

Increase heat to medium high. Stir in sugar snap peas and corn. Cook, stirring constantly, 3-4 minutes more, or until sugar snap peas are bright green and crisp-tender.

Remove from heat, stir in chopped basil and mini-mozzarella balls. Serve immediately.

Hot Carrots

2 pounds of fresh carrots, peeled and cut into pieces on diagonal
1 12 ounces can whole jalapeños with juice
2 onions, sliced
2 tablespoons oil
1 cup vinegar preferably raw apple cider vinegar
Salt and pepper to taste

In boiling water, cook carrots to desired tenderness. Don't overcook; they should still be crisp. Drain.

In large glass bowl or glass jar combine carrots, jalapeños and juice, onions, oil, vinegar, and salt and pepper to taste. Chill at least three hours.

Sweet Potato Chips

Sprinkle slices of sweet potatoes with salt, cinnamon, sugar or chili powder. Spread out onto baking sheet and bake at 400 F till crisp.

Spinach Pesto
(makes 1⅓ cups)

3 cups fresh spinach leaves (4 ounces)
1 clove garlic, minced
½ cup olive oil, or more to taste
2 tablespoons dried basil
1 tablespoon dried oregano
¼ cup parmesan cheese (optional)
¼ cup walnuts
3 tablespoons raw sunflower seeds

In food processor or blender, combine all ingredients. Blend well.

Basic Fried Green Tomatoes
(serves 8)

½ cup whole wheat flour
½ teaspoon salt
½ tablespoon freshly ground pepper
2 tablespoons cold soy milk
3 tablespoons olive oil
4 green tomatoes, sliced ¼ inch thick
¼ cup minced fresh dill, chives or basil
2 lemons, cut into wedges

In a small bowl, combine the flour, salt and pepper. Pour the milk into another small bowl.

In a large skillet, heat the oil over medium heat. Dip each tomato slice into the milk then into the flour. Fry the slices in hot oil until golden (about 5 minutes) turning over once or twice. Drain on paper towels.

Garnish with herbs and serve immediately with lemon wedges.

Un-fried French Fried Potatoes

5 large baking potatoes sliced like French fries
Olive oil spray (comes in a spray can)
2 large egg whites
1 tablespoon Cajun spice (optional)

Preheat oven to 400 F.

Spray baking sheet with spray very well.

Combine egg whites and Cajun spice in a bowel. Mix potatoes well into the egg whites to coat. Spread them onto the baking sheet evenly. Place the baking sheet on the bottom shelf of the oven. Bake for 40-45 minutes, until the fries are crispy, turning them every 6-8 minutes with a pancake turner to brown evenly. Salt to taste after they are cooked.

Toast for Breakfast

1 slice whole wheat bread toasted

Puncture holes in toast with a fork. Pour 1 tablespoon flax oil and sprinkle just a little salt. Tastes just like buttered toast.

Celery and Peanut Butter

Take ribs of celery and spread nutty peanut butter and enjoy as snack.

Split Pea Medley
(serves 6)

---

1 medium onion, chopped (about 1 cup)
4 cloves of garlic, minced
1 tablespoon olive oil
1 lemon peel, 3x1 inch strip
3 tablespoons thyme
2 tablespoons crushed dried bay leaf
2 cups vegetable or chicken broth
1 cup water
¾ cup dried green split peas
⅛ teaspoon pepper
3 ribs celery, cut diagonally into ½ inch slices (about 1 cup)
1 cup carrots, cut into ½ inch chunks
½ cup peas
Lemon wedges and fresh thyme for garnish (optional)
Salt to taste

In large sauce pan, sauté onions and garlic in oil with lemon peel, thyme, and bay leaf for 4-5 minutes, stirring constantly. Add broth, water, split peas and pepper; bring to a boil. Reduce heat; cover and simmer for 45 minutes. Add salt.

Remove lemon peel. Add celery and carrots; cover and cook until vegetables are just tender (10-15 minutes). Garnish each serving with lemon wedges and fresh thyme if desired.

Corn Chowder

1½ cup cooked brown rice
6-8 cups water
2 cups corn
¾ teaspoons olive or sesame oil
4-5 ribs celery, chopped
4 cloves garlic, minced
4 medium potatoes, cubed
1 large onion, chopped
Salt to taste

In a blender, blend the cooked rice with 2 cups water until smooth. Place rice mixture with 4 cups water in large soup pot and bring to boil. Add the potatoes, celery, onions, salt and add more water if needed. Reduce heat and simmer until tender (about 15 minutes).

Add garlic, corn and oil. Heat and serve.

Sweet Potato Coconut Soup

2 large onions, diced
3 ribs of celery, cut into ¼ inch slices
¼ cup of ginger, grated
1 medium carrot, cut into ¼ inch slices
3 cups sweet potatoes, peeled and cut into 1 inch cubes
1 can of coconut milk
¼ cup all natural maple syrup or sweetener of choice
Salt to taste
Hot pepper sauce and scallions (garnish)

Sauté onions over medium heat until they become caramelized. Add celery and ginger and sauté for one minute.

Add carrots and sweet potatoes. Cover with water and simmer until soft. Add the coconut milk, maple syrup, and salt and bring to a boil. Pour mixture into a blender and blend until very smooth. Garnish with a swirl of your favorite hot pepper sauce and chopped green onions.

Corn and Sweet Potato Soup

1 red onion, chopped
½ cup chopped celery
2 teaspoons minced garlic
1 green bell pepper, chopped
2 cups diced, peeled sweet potato (yam)
1 16 ounce can corn
1 15 ounce can cream-style corn
1 10 ounce can chopped tomatoes and green chilis
1 6 ounce can tomato paste
4 cups vegetable or chicken broth
Salt and pepper taste
Sliced green onions (optional)

Coat a large pot with non-stick cooking spray, and sauté the onion, celery, and green pepper until tender. Add the sweet potato, corn, cream-style corn, tomatoes and green chilis, tomato paste and broth; bring the mixture to a boil. Season with salt and pepper; and add garlic. Garnish with green onions, if desired, and serve.

Baked Pumpkin Soup
(serves 4)

1 4 pound pumpkin
1 onion, chopped
1 inch cube fresh ginger root grated
3 tablespoons extra virgin olive oil
1 zucchini, sliced
4 ounces sliced mushrooms
1 14 ounce can chopped tomatoes
1 cup whole wheat pasta shells (the small ones)
2 cups vegetable or chicken broth
Salt and ground black pepper to taste
4 tablespoons ricotta cheese
3 tablespoons basil

Preheat the oven to 350 F. Cut the top off the pumpkin with a large, sharp knife, then scoop out and discard all the seeds.

Using a small, sharp knife and a sturdy tablespoon extract as much of the pumpkin flesh as possible, then chop it into chunks.

Bake the pumpkin with its lid on for 45 minutes to one hour until the inside begins to soften.

Meanwhile, make the filling. Gently fry the onion, ginger and pumpkin flesh in the olive oil for about 10 minutes, stirring occasionally.

Add the zucchini and mushrooms and cook for another 3 minutes, then stir in the tomatoes, pasta shells and stock. Season well, bring to a boil, then cover and simmer gently for 10 minutes.

Stir the ricotta cheese and basil into the pasta and spoon the mixture into the pumpkin. It may not be possible to fit all the filling into the pumpkin shell, so serve the rest separately if this is the case.

Delicious Vegetable Chowder
(serves 6)

1 tablespoon olive oil
½ cup finely chopped onion
2 cups cooked long grain brown rice, cooked with
   1 chicken or vegetable bouillon cube
½ teaspoon dry mustard
1 cup peeled, chopped carrots
1 cup chopped zucchini
1½ cups potatoes, peeled and chopped
Salt and pepper to taste
2 cups corn
2 teaspoon dried basil

Heat oil over medium heat in large saucepan. Add onion, and cook, stirring often, 8-9 minutes, or until softened. Add mustard, 1 cup water, and cooked rice. Puree until smooth then return to pot. Add remaining vegetables, salt and pepper. Cover and cook 10 minutes or until vegetables are tender. Stir in corn, and basil, and cook until heated through. If you need to add more water do so. Serve.

Lentil Soup

8 cups chicken or vegetable stock
1 cup brown lentils
1 onion, chopped
2 carrots, sliced
½ tablespoon salt
1 small yam, cubed
4 cloves garlic, minced
2 celery ribs, sliced
1 teaspoon basil
1 tablespoon tamari

Bring broth to a boil in large soup pot. Add lentils to boiling water, then cover, lower heat and simmer for 20 minutes. Add onion, celery, carrots, yam, basil, salt and tamari. Bring back to a boil. Cover and reduce heat to a simmer another 5-10 minutes until vegetables are tender. Add garlic. Serve.

Portuguese Soup
(serves 4-6)

———◆———

1 cup chopped onions
½ tablespoon olive oil
1 cup diced carrots
1 35 ounce can Italian tomatoes or one pound
   fresh tomatoes, chopped
1 cup vegetable juices, fresh or V-8
1 teaspoon salt
¼ teaspoon black pepper
1 teaspoon basil
1 teaspoon thyme
2 bay leaves, crushed
4 cloves smashed
¼ cup slivered almonds (garnish)

Brown chopped onions in olive oil. Add other ingredients and simmer, covered for 20 minutes or until carrots are tender. Add garlic. Sprinkle with slivered almonds.

Chunky Potato Soup
(serves 4-6)

2½ cups of cooking water mixed with 2 vegetable bouillon or chicken cubes
½ cup sliced, celery
1 cup onions, chopped
½ cup sliced carrots
5 cups sliced, unpeeled potatoes
2 teaspoons salt
½ teaspoon dry mustard
2 cups soy milk
1 teaspoon dried parsley flakes

Place first 5 ingredients in a 2½ quart saucepan and bring to a boil. Reduce heat and simmer, covered, until celery and carrots are tender. Mash mixture slightly in the saucepan with a potato masher. Add remaining ingredients and bring soup to a boil again. Reduce heat to simmer and continue to cook, stirring, about 2 minutes more.

Quick White Bean Soup
(serves 6-8)

6 tablespoons olive oil
1 rib celery, finely chopped
1 onion, finely chopped
1 carrot, finely chopped
1 clove garlic smashed
3 cups cooked white navy or cannellini beans
6 cups vegetable or chicken broth
2 teaspoons salt
1 teaspoon freshly ground black pepper
2 plum tomatoes, finely chopped
2 tablespoons rosemary

Heat 2 tablespoons of olive oil in a large saucepan over medium heat. Add celery, onion, carrot and garlic, and cook until they are softened. Puree half the white beans with vegetable stock and remaining 4 tablespoons of olive oil. Season with salt and pepper to taste. Add tomatoes and rosemary to vegetables, and heat through. Pour 1 cup of white bean puree into a soup bowl. Spoon 2 tablespoons of vegetables into center of bowl. Spoon 2 tablespoons of remaining white beans over vegetables. Add garlic. Repeat until all ingredients are used up.

Jeff's Favorite Minestrone Soup

Chicken or vegetable broth as needed to make soup
3 carrots, sliced
2 zucchini, sliced
3 ribs celery, sliced thin
4 cups shredded cabbage
l large can stewed tomatoes
3 cups cooked small macaroni shell
1 can kidney beans or cook your own
3 cups cooked garbanzo beans
3 rounded tablespoons Italian seasoning
Salt to taste
4 cloves garlic, crushed

Cook carrots till slightly tender. Add other vegetables, seasonings and cook till tender. Add everything else and mix well. Serve.

Chickpea, Lentils and Bulgur Wheat Soup
(serves 8)

½ cup bulgur wheat
½ cup uncooked lentils
1½ cups canned chickpeas, drained and rinsed or
   cook your own
Juice of 1 lemon
1 tablespoon red pepper paste
4 cloves garlic, crushed
Salt and ground black pepper to taste

Bring 4 cups of water mixed with 2 vegetable or chicken bouillon cubes, to a boil over medium heat. Stir in the bulgur wheat and lentils, cover the pan, reduce the heat to low and cook for about 15 minutes, stirring occasionally, until tender.

Add the chickpeas, lemon juice, red pepper paste, garlic, salt and pepper. Add liquid according to your desire, stirring well, and cook for 5 more minutes, or until heated through.

Barley Soup
(serves 6)

———◆———

1 red onion, sliced
½ fennel bulb, sliced
2 ribs of celery chopped
2 carrots, chopped
1 parsnip, sliced
3 tablespoons sunflower or olive oil
1 cup pearl barley
4 cups chicken or vegetable broth
2 tablespoon garlic salt
2 teaspoons dried thyme
Fresh parsley, chopped, to garnish
Salt and ground black pepper to taste
⅔ cup green beans, sliced
1 15 ounce can pinto beans, drained or cook your own

In a large, heatproof casserole bowl, sauté the onion, fennel, carrots, celery, green beans and parsnip gently in the oil for 10 minutes.

Stir in the barley and broth. Bring to a boil, add the herbs and seasoning, then cover and simmer gently for 40 minutes.

Stir in pinto beans and heat.

Ladle the barley into bowls and serve sprinkled with parsley.

Curried Kale Salad

Dressing:
1 cup orange juice
1 tablespoon marjoram
1 tablespoon oregano
2 cloves garlic
1 small piece fresh ginger (½ inch piece)
¼ teaspoon cayenne pepper
½ teaspoon curry powder
¼ teaspoon salt
½ cup raw pumpkin seeds

Blend first 8 ingredients until smooth. Add pumpkin seeds. Blend until smooth.

Salad:
1 bunch kale (dinosaur is best), remove stems and cut fine
1-2 large tomatoes, diced
¼ red onion, chopped

Toss dressing with the salad ingredients and marinate for 3-4 hours or eat right away. What a great way to eat kale. Yum!

Summer Pasta Salad with Grilled Vegetables

(serves 8)

8 ounces rotini, shells or other short whole wheat pasta
3 tablespoons extra virgin olive oil
2 tablespoons red wine vinegar
2 cloves garlic, minced
Salt and freshly ground black pepper to taste
1 cup cherry tomatoes
2 medium sized zucchini, chopped
1 red bell pepper, chopped
1 bunch of red scallions, trimmed and chopped
1 cup black olives
2 tablespoons oregano
2 tablespoons basil
1 cup mushrooms, dried or fresh, chopped

Prepare medium-hot charcoal fire or preheat gas grill (or broiler). Remember you can use the broiler in your stove and it works very well for this recipe.

Bring large pot of lightly salted water to a boil. Add pasta, and cook until al dente, about 7 minutes. Drain and rinse thoroughly to cool. Transfer to large bowl, and toss with 1 tablespoon olive oil.

Whisk together remaining olive oil, vinegar, garlic, spices, salt and pepper in 9x13 inch baking dish. Add tomatoes, mushrooms, zucchini, red pepper and scallions, and toss to coat with oil mixture. Place under broiler and roast till browned. Turn vegetables with a pancake turner periodically.

When the vegetables are done, let them stand until cool enough to handle.

Add vegetables to pasta. Add olives and toss well.

Roxanne's Favorite Yum Yum Salad

2 cups crushed pineapple
Juice of 1 lemon
2 envelopes of Knox gelatin
½ cup mild cheese, grated
½ pint whipping cream or non dairy whipped topping
½ cup raw sugar

Heat pineapple, sugar and lemon juice until sugar is dissolved. Soak gelatin in ½ cup cold water for 5 minutes. Add to hot mixture. When cool and beginning to set, add grated cheese and whipping cream. Beat till stiff. Chill.

Dawn's Famous Potato Salad

7 red potatoes, cubed
1 large red onion, finely chopped
½ cup mayonnaise
½ cup black olives, sliced
¼ cup soy Baco Bits (soy based bacon substitute)
¼ cup mustard
3 eggs, hard boiled and chopped
Salt and pepper to taste

Bring water to a boil and boil potatoes until slightly soft. Mix mustard, mayonnaise, salt and pepper and combine with potatoes, onion, eggs, olives and soy Baco Bits. Chill. Sprinkle paprika on top for color.

Spinach-Pine Nut Salad
(4-6 servings)

2 bunches fresh spinach, washed and stemmed
1 red onion, sliced thinly
½ cup grated carrot
½ cup pine nuts
½ cup olives, pitted
1 cup crumbled part-skim feta cheese
2 tablespoons olive oil
1 tablespoon wine vinegar
1 teaspoon lemon juice
1 teaspoon Dijon mustard
Salt and pepper to taste

In a large salad bowl, mix the spinach leaves, onion, carrot, pine nuts, olives and feta cheese.

In another bowl, whisk together the olive oil, wine vinegar, lemon juice, Dijon mustard, and salt and pepper to taste.

Pour the dressing over the salad and toss to combine. Serve immediately.

Coleslaw
(8-10 servings)

---

1 head cabbage, shredded
1 medium green bell pepper, diced
2 tablespoons chopped pimiento
½ teaspoon celery seeds
¼ teaspoon pepper
1 teaspoon raw sugar
1 teaspoon lemon juice
¼ cup raw apple cider vinegar
½ cup soy sour cream
½ cup mayonnaise
Salt to taste

In large bowl, combine the cabbage, green bell pepper, chopped pimiento, celery seeds, pepper, sugar, vinegar, soy sour cream and mayonnaise. Stir ingredients to mix well. Salt and serve.

Couscous Salad

- 1 cup couscous
- ¼ cup extra virgin olive oil
- 2 red or green jalapeño peppers, seeded and minced—if desired
- 1 teaspoon ground cumin
- 1 teaspoon ground coriander
- 4 cloves garlic, crushed
- Salt to taste
- 2 cups baby peas
- 2 chopped tomatoes
- 1 packed cup fresh mint leaves, coarsely chopped
- 6 thin scallions, thinly sliced
- 1 lemon for zest and juice
- 6 ounces crumbled feta cheese
- Tender lettuce leaves
- ½ cup chopped olives

Combine couscous, 1 tablespoon oil, jalapeños, cumin, coriander, garlic and salt to taste in large bowl; whisk together until couscous is evenly coated. Scatter peas on top, and pour on 2 cups boiling water.

Cover bowl with plastic wrap. Let stand for 5 minutes, until water is absorbed. Uncover bowl, fluff mixture with fork and cool completely.

Meanwhile, combine tomatoes, mint and scallions. Grate about 1½ teaspoons zest from lemon on top.

Add cooled couscous mixture to tomato mixture with remaining 3 tablespoons oil, juice of half lemon or to taste and salt to taste. Toss to combine including cheese.

Line 6 plates with lettuce leaves, and top with salad. Garnish with olives, and serve.

Orzo Primavera Salad

(6-8 servings)

8 ounces orzo (rice-shaped pasta)
½ diced zucchini, blanched*
½ cup diced carrots, blanched*
1 cup corn
½ cup parsley
1 cup frozen baby peas, thawed
½ cup thinly sliced radishes
¼ cup chopped red onion

Cook orzo in boiling water according to package directions until al dente. Drain in a colander and rinse briefly under running cold water. Shake the colander gently to drain completely and set aside.

Dressing:
¼ cup fresh lemon juice
1½ teaspoons grated lemon zest
2 cloves garlic, minced
Salt and ground black pepper to taste
⅓ to ½ cup extra virgin olive oil
¼ cup loosely packed fresh basil leaves, cup into thin strips or 2 tablespoons of dried basil

In a small bowl, stir together the lemon juice and zest, garlic, and salt and pepper to taste. Gradually whisk in the olive oil until an emulsion forms. Stir in the basil.

Place the orzo in a large serving bowl and add the zucchini, carrots, peas, radishes, parsley, corn and onion. Toss gently. Add dressing and toss again. Serve immediately.

*Note: to blanch vegetables, plunge them into boiling water for one to two minutes, then into ice water.

Baby Pea Salad
(serves 8)

---

2 10 ounce packages of frozen tiny peas
1 cup soy sour cream
1 tablespoon dried dill weed
2 teaspoons chopped chives
1 teaspoon curry powder
Juice of ½ lemon
Salt and pepper to taste
Crisp salad greens for serving

Cook the peas according to directions on package; drain thoroughly. In a bowl, mix together soy sour cream, dill, chives, curry powder, lemon juice and salt and pepper to taste. Carefully combine with peas. Chill and serve on a bed of crisp salad greens. Garnish with more dill or chives if desired.

Pasta Salad with Peanut Dressing

1¼ pound corkscrew pasta, cooked al dente
½ cup cucumber, peeled, thinly sliced
1 green bell pepper, thinly sliced
½ cup tomato, thinly sliced
½ cup scallions, minced
¼ cup parsley, chopped fine
4 tablespoons raw cashews, chopped
Pinch of red chili flakes (optional)
Salt to taste
Ground pepper to taste
Fresh cilantro to garnish

Peanut dressing:

2 tablespoons peanut butter
½ teaspoon whole grain mustard or Dijon mustard
2 teaspoons Bragg's liquid aminos
1 tablespoon raw sugar
2 tablespoons raw apple cider vinegar or wine vinegar
1 teaspoon red wine vinegar
2 teaspoons cilantro, minced
¼ teaspoon fresh ginger, grated
⅓ cup salad oil or virgin olive oil
Salt to taste
Fresh ground pepper to taste

Prepare peanut dressing by combining all ingredients and mixing well. Adjust the seasoning and reserve.

Prepare pasta and salad ingredients, combine in a large bowl. Add enough peanut dressing to lightly coat the pasta and vegetables. Season with salt and pepper to taste, toss. Incorporate more dressing if needed.

Millet Grain Salad

1 tablespoon sesame or sunflower oil
1 carrot, grated
1 cup sliced celery or julienned zucchini
¼ cup parsley, chopped
2-3 cups cooked millet*

Spicy Sesame Sauce:
2 tablespoons tamari or sea salt
2 tablespoons water
dash of cayenne pepper
2 tablespoons raw tahini
¼ teaspoons sesame oil

In small bowl, stir together the tahini with water until very smooth. Stir in the tamari, sesame oil and cayenne until very well combined.

Heat oil in large frying pan or wok over high heat until oil is hot but not smoking. Stir fry the carrot and celery or zucchini until vegetables are tender (about 3 minutes). Pour in the water and cover for a minute. Add the millet, parsley and spicy sesame sauce. Toss and serve hot or cold.

*You can use any cooked grain, such as basmati rice, couscous, barley, etc.

You can vary the flavor of the sauce by adding some of the following: 1 teaspoon toasted sesame seeds, ½ teaspoon vinegar, ½ teaspoon sorghum syrup, ¼ teaspoon grated ginger, ¼ teaspoon minced garlic, 1 teaspoon, cilantro.

Cranberry Waldorf Salad
(10 servings)

1 tablespoon (1½ envelopes) unflavored gelatin
2 cups apple juice (divided use)
1 12 ounce bag fresh cranberries
⅔ cup raw sugar
1 Granny Smith apple, peeled, cored and chopped
1 medium celery rib, chopped
½ cup coarsely chopped walnuts

In a small bowl sprinkle gelatin over ½ cup of apple juice; set aside. In large saucepan, mix cranberries, remaining 1½ cups apple juice and sugar. Bring to a boil over medium high heat, stirring often to dissolve sugar. Cook until all the cranberries have popped, about 5 minutes. Reduce the heat to very low. Stir in gelatin and continue stirring until gelatin is completely dissolved (1-2 minutes). Transfer mixture to a large bowl. Refrigerate until cool and partially thickened (about 2 hours). A spoon drawn through the mixture should leave an impression.

Lightly oil a 5 cup mold. Stir apple, celery, and walnuts into cranberry mixture. Pour into prepared mold and cover with plastic wrap. Refrigerate until completely set at least 8 hours). Can be prepared up to 2 days in advance.

To serve: Fill a large bowl with hot water. Dip mold, just to top edge, into water and hold for 5 seconds. Remove from water and dry mold. Remove plastic wrap. Invert mold onto platter, holding mold and platter together. Shake until salad releases. Cut into wedges and serve.

Chef's Spinach Salad
(serves 5)

1 pound raw spinach
1 cup chick peas, cooked
½ cup sliced mushrooms
½ cup sliced beets
8 ounces farmer or feta cheese
½ cup raw pumpkin or sunflower seeds
2 tablespoons virgin olive oil
Juice of 1 lemon
Salt and pepper to taste

Wash spinach and tear into bite sized pieces. Toss chick peas, mushrooms, beets, and crumbled farmer or feta cheese with spinach. Just before serving sprinkle on seeds and add lemon juice, salt, pepper and oil as a dressing.

Delicious Salad

½ head chopped kale, vein removed
½ head chopped romaine
2 chopped tomatoes
½ cup chopped parsley, stems removed
1 tablespoon caraway
½ teaspoon anise
2 tablespoons virgin olive oil
3 teaspoons lemon juice
2 cloves chopped or smashed garlic
Salt to taste

Mix spices, oil, lemon juice, salt and smashed garlic. Add to all of the vegetables, mix well.

Kashi Vegetable Salad

2 cups of Kashi, cooked and cold
½ cup mushrooms, chopped
¼ green pepper, diced
¼ red pepper, diced
1 chopped zucchini
1 chopped yellow squash
1 8 ounce can water chestnuts, drained and chopped
¼ cup parsley, chopped
¼ cup green onions, diced
¼ cup tomatoes, diced
½ cup olive oil
½ cup Bragg's liquid aminos
3 tablespoons wine vinegar
2 teaspoons Dijon mustard
1 rib celery, chopped

Mix together lightly in large serving bowl Kashi, mushrooms, peppers, water chestnuts, parsley, onions, celery, tomatoes (any choice of fresh chopped vegetables may be used). Stir together the oil, liquid aminos, wine vinegar, and Dijon mustard. Salt if desired. Pour dressing over Kashi to taste and toss. Refrigerate well.

Tabbouleh

(serves 4)

1 cup bulgur wheat
6 tablespoons fresh lemon juice
5 tablespoons extra virgin olive oil
1 cup fresh parsley, chopped (remove stems)—pressed down
3 scallions, finely chopped
4 firm tomatoes, skinned and chopped
1 cup chopped cilantro
Salt and ground black pepper to taste

Cover the bulgur with boiling water and soak for 20 minutes, then drain well and squeeze out even more water from it with your hands.

Put the bulgur into another bowl and add all other ingredients, stirring and seasoning well.

Cover and chill for a few hours, or overnight, if possible.

Caesar's Salad
(serves 4)

Croutons as you desire
1 romaine lettuce, washed and torn in pieces
½ cup parmesan cheese

Dressing:
2 eggs
2 tablespoons extra virgin olive oil
2 teaspoons mustard
2 teaspoons Worcestershire sauce
2 tablespoons fresh lemon juice
2 garlic cloves crushed

Toss torn lettuce sprinkling between the leaves with the cheese. Cover and set aside.

Boil water in a small saucepan and cook the eggs for 1 minute only. Remove the eggs, and crack them open into a jug or bowl. The whites should be milky and the yolks raw.

Whisk the dressing ingredients into the eggs. When ready to serve pour the dressing over the leaves, toss well together and serve topped with the croutons.

Millan's Beet Apple Salad

Grate l beet and grate 1 apple (equal sizes) or grate in food processor and mix together with 1 tablespoon lemon juice.

Roxanne's Popular Broccoli Salad

Sauce:
1 cup mayonnaise
¼ cup raw sugar
2 tablespoons raw apple cider vinegar

Salad:
1 bunch of broccoli, diced
1 small red onion, diced
1 pound Fakin' (soy) Bacon, cooked and crumbled or Baco Bits
½ cup golden raisins, chopped
1 cup raw sunflower seeds

Mix above ingredients with sauce.

Kale Delight

1 head of kale or chard
Juice of one lemon
Salt to taste
2 cloves garlic, crushed
¼ cup virgin olive oil
¼ cup red onion, chopped very fine

Remove vein of kale or chard. Tear leaves into small, bite-size pieces.

Mix lemon, salt, garlic, olive oil, and onion together first. Then add to kale or chard. Massage the greens well with clean hands. You should feel the texture change and the volume should appear smaller. Marinate in a glass container, in the refrigerator, for 4 hours or overnight. Delicious!

Marinated Cucumber Salad
(Serves 2-4)

Salad:

3 cups peeled cucumbers, chopped
2 apples, cored and chopped
1 cup celery hearts (inner ribs), diced
20 pitted Italian olives, sliced

Combine in a bowl.

Dressing:

½ cup water
2 tablespoons grated carrot
1 teaspoon chopped celery
½ teaspoon salt
½ teaspoon kelp granules
½ small avocado

Blend all till smooth and add to the salad ingredients. Keeps for 3-4 days, disappears in minutes!

Theresa's Nopales Salad
Delicious Cactus Salad

2-3 nopales (cactus leaves—smaller, young leaves are more tender and tasty)
2 tomatoes, chopped
2 green onions, chopped
1 cup cilantro, stems removed—chopped
1-2 serrano chilis (optional)
1 tablespoon virgin olive oil
2 tablespoons lemon juice
2 tablespoons Mexican seasoning (or to taste)
2 teaspoons garlic salt (or to taste)

Trim/scrape off needles and thorns and dice.

Place nopales in pot covered with cold water. When water boils, remove from heat. Rinse completely with cold water for 3 minutes to remove stickiness of cactus.

Place in new water to cover. Bring to boil and boil for 3 minutes adding salt and spices of your choice.

Remove from burner. Empty water and fill again with cold water to cool. Then remove cactus and add the chopped vegetables and lemon juice.

Mix with Mexican seasoning, garlic salt and olive oil. Chill 30 minutes and serve in corn or whole wheat tortillas.

Leek Quiche
(serves 6-8)

Easy to make yet satisfying. Serve with spinach salad tossed with fresh apple slivers, chopped walnuts and olive oil vinaigrette.

Filling:
1½ cups sliced leeks
½ cup sliced mushrooms
3 tablespoons butter
3 egg whites
1½ cups soy milk
6 ounces grated Swiss cheese
Salt and pepper to taste
1 rounded tablespoon Spike seasoning

Pie crust: purchase a frozen, whole wheat crust from your market

Filling:
Sauté the leeks and mushrooms in 3 tablespoons of butter until tender but not brown. Spread the mixture out evenly over the bottom of the unbaked pie crust. In a medium bowl beat together the eggs and soy milk, stir in the cheese, and seasonings. Pour over the leeks and bake for 30 minutes at 325 F until golden brown and firmly set in the middle.

Potato-Spinach Bake
(serves 6)

───◆───

1 large baking potato (about ½ pound), rinsed and unpeeled
Salt and pepper to taste
1 cup uncooked quick-cooking barley or regular barley
   you have cooked
2 bunches of spinach (about 20 ounces), trimmed and rinsed
2½ cups low-fat shredded cheddar cheese
2 large roasted bell peppers, cut into strips (place under
   broiler turning once to brown each side)
1 cup marinara or spaghetti sauce for garnish, mixed with
   2 tablespoons of Italian seasonings.

Preheat the oven to 450 F. Spray 9-inch deep dish pie plate with non-stick cooking spray. Bring 2 cups of water to a boil.

Slice potato into ¼ inch thick slices, and place around bottom of pie plate in a single layer. Spray potato slices lightly with non-stick cooking spray, season with salt and pepper, and bake.

Meanwhile, cook barley according to package directions, drain and place in large mixing bowl. Be sure the spinach is rinsed very carefully because of the dirt on leaves. Cut spinach width wise into large pieces, and, using water clinging to leaves, steam spinach in covered pot until wilted, 2-3 minutes. Remove from heat, drain and press out excess water. Combine with barley in a mixing bowl. Add 2 cups shredded cheese, and toss together.

Place bell pepper strips on potato slices. Mound barley mixture on top of pepper strips, sprinkle top with remaining ½ cup cheese and bake until cheese bubbles and browns.

Remove from heat, slice and serve with marinara sauce.

Curried Barley with Portobello Mushrooms

(serves 4)

4 large Portobello mushroom caps
½ cup uncooked quick cooking barley
2 tablespoons vegetable oil
1 onion diced
1 tablespoon minced garlic, or to taste
1 bell pepper, diced
1 teaspoon curry powder
1 teaspoon ground cumin
Salt to taste
½ cup nonfat plain soy yogurt

Preheat the oven to 400 F.

Remove the steams from the mushrooms, clean off dirt and chop the stems. Set aside. Scrape away the gills from the underside of the caps, spray the tops of the caps with nonstick cooking spray and put the caps into a large baking pan, rounded side up. Bake for about 10 minutes, or until the tops are tender to the touch.

Meanwhile, cook the barley in 1 cup of boiling water or according to package directions. Heat the oil in a large skillet over medium heat, and sauté the onion and pepper for about 5 minutes, or until the onion starts to turn translucent. Stir in the curry powder, cumin and salt, and reduce heat to low. Remove the mushroom caps from the oven, turn them over so gill sides are facing up and set aside.

Add the cooked barley and yogurt to the skillet, and stir. Continue to cook for 5 minutes more. Remove from the heat, add garlic, then spoon equal amounts of the barley mixture into the caps and serve.

Potato and Caramelized Onion Tart

2 large Idaho potatoes (about 9 ounces) peeled and thinly sliced
6 tablespoons (¾ a stick) butter, melted (divided use)
1 teaspoon seasoned salt
2 large onions, thinly sliced
1 teaspoon raw sugar
1 cup shredded Swiss cheese
½ cup dry bread crumbs (plain or seasoned)

Preheat oven to 375 F. In a small bowl, toss potato slices with 1 tablespoon of the melted butter and the salt. Arrange the slices in a 10 inch tart pan with removable bottom, or 10 inch pie pan. Bake for 20 minutes.

While potatoes are baking, sauté the onions in a medium skillet over medium heat in 3 tablespoons of the melted butter until soft and beginning to brown (about 5 minutes). Turn the heat down to low, sprinkle the onions with the sugar and continue to cook until onions are deep brown, but not burned or crispy (about 10 minutes).

When potatoes are done, remove from the oven (leave oven on) and spread the onion mixture over them. Sprinkle the top with the cheese.

In a small bowl, combine the bread crumbs with the remaining 2 tablespoons of melted butter and sprinkle the mixture over the cheese. Return the tart to the oven to bake an additional 10-15 minutes, until the cheese is melted and crumb topping is golden brown. Remove from the oven and let tart cool for 5 minutes before serving.

Calabacitas

1 bell pepper, chopped
2 cups sliced zucchini
1 medium onion, chopped
4 cloves smashed garlic
2 fresh tomatoes, chopped
1 can of corn
½ cup fresh cilantro, chopped
1 jalapeño, finely chopped, optional
2 teaspoon Mexican seasonings
Salt to taste
½ cup grated Jack cheese

Sauté onions. Add everything else except the garlic and cilantro. Simmer until the zucchini is tender. Then add smashed garlic and cilantro. Spread in baking dish. Lay Jack cheese on top. Broil until cheese is slightly melted. Serve.

Millan's Vegetable Stir Fry

Use the following vegetables in equal amounts depending on how many servings.

Zucchini
Can water chestnuts
Broccoli
Shredded Cabbage
Cauliflower
Mushrooms
Bean sprouts
Celery
Carrots

Chop vegetables to bite size.

Sauté carrots for 5 minutes in olive oil. Add all of the above vegetables. Sauté for another five minutes. In a cup place one rounded tablespoon corn starch. Slowly stir in one cup chicken broth to mix well. (Use Better Than Bouillon brand.) Add this to vegetables. Cook vegetables till tender and liquid thickens. You may need to add water if it gets too thick. Then add Bragg's liquid aminos to taste. Soy sauce will also work. Place stir fry on steamed brown rice. Enjoy!

USE A WOK TO PREPARE THIS DISH. IF YOU DON'T HAVE ONE BUY ONE. YOU WILL LOVE IT.

Millan's Vegetarian Enchiladas
(My Grandmother's Recipe)

2 heads chopped spinach
2 medium zucchini, sliced
2 yellow squash, sliced
2 medium bell peppers, sliced
1½ cup mushrooms, sliced
2 large onions, diced
1 7 ounce can whole green chilis, chopped

Mix above vegetables, then set aside.

Mix thoroughly:
1 cup virgin olive oil
4½ ounces chopped garlic (comes in a jar)
3 teaspoons Spike or season salt
3 tablespoons Mexican seasoning
3 tablespoons oregano

Stir above oil and seasonings into above vegetables. Mix well. Spread into shallow baking pan. Place under broiler. Broil until slightly brown, then stir and broil again until most vegetables are slightly browned.

1 28 ounce can mild red enchilada sauce
3 tablespoon corn starch
1 dozen corn tortillas
3 cups of mixed Monterey Jack cheese and mild cheddar cheese, grated
1 to 2 cans black olives, chopped, but not too fine
2 to 4 tablespoons of olive oil

Mix the three tablespoons corn starch into approximately 2 tablespoons of the enchilada sauce, stir to mix smoothly. Then stir completely into the 28 ounce can of enchilada sauce for a nice thickening effect.

(continued on next page)

Heat 2 tablespoons of olive oil in a large skillet. Using a prong, fry slightly both sides of each corn tortilla. Place fried tortillas on paper towels to drain oil. You may need to replenish oil as you continue to fry the corn tortillas.

Using the prongs, dip completely one of the fried corn tortillas into enchilada sauce, then lay flat on a large baking plate. Spread approximately 4 tablespoons of the vegetables evenly on top of tortilla. Sprinkle rounded tablespoons of chopped olives, then 2 to 3 tablespoons of cheese on top of tortilla as well.

Repeat until all corn tortillas are lying on top of each other. You will need two plates as the piles get quite high. Pour the rest of the enchilada sauce on top of the last enchilada of each plate. You may freeze one plate for future. Bake for 15 minutes at 375 F.

Vegetable Patties

2 to 3 tablespoons olive oil
1½ cups chopped onion
3 cloves minced garlic
Salt & pepper to taste
2 tablespoons Spike seasonings
4 cups grated carrots
½ cup chopped walnuts
2 cups frozen baby peas
1½ cups bread crumbs (take two slices of bread and run them through grating blade of food processor to make bread crumbs)
3 large eggs
½ cup soy milk

Sauté onion and carrots in half of oil till tender. Add walnuts, baby peas, bread crumbs and seasonings and mix together. Beat eggs and then add soy milk to eggs. Add garlic then mix all ingredients together. Make flat patties about 4 inches in diameter and sauté in rest of oil till brown on each side.

Eggplant Parmesan
(serves 2)

———◆———

1 medium eggplant, about ¾ a pound
2 eggs, beaten
1 cup Italian-style breadcrumbs
¾ cup olive oil
15 ounces ricotta cheese
1 14 ounce jar spaghetti sauce, with 4 cloves crushed garlic
6 ounces mozzarella cheese, sliced
4 teaspoon Italian herb seasoning
½ cup grated parmesan cheese

Cut eggplant crosswise into half-inch slices. Dip slices into beaten eggs, then into breadcrumbs. Coat completely, but shake off excess crumbs. Slowly heat oil in large frying pan. Sauté eggplant until lightly browned, about 2 minutes each side; drain on paper towel. Preheat oven to 350 F. To fill two individual baking dishes: make two layers of ingredients in each dish, starting with eggplant and continuing in order listed (ricotta cheese, sauce, mozzarella cheese, seasoning, parmesan cheese). Each layer will have ¼ of the ingredients. Bake, uncovered, for 20 minutes.

Vegetable Lasagna
(serves 8-10 kids)

2 heads of chopped spinach
1 cup of sliced mushrooms
4 rounded tablespoons of Italian seasonings
1 jar marinara sauce
4 cloves garlic, minced
1 medium zucchini, chopped
1 bell pepper, chopped
1 teaspoon oregano
2 tablespoons olive oil
1½ cup ricotta cheese
1 cup shredded mozzarella cheese
½ cup parmesan cheese
8 ounce package lasagna noodles

Lightly sauté vegetables in olive oil. Combine marinara with vegetables, Italian seasoning and oregano and simmer for 8-10 minutes till tender. Mix in garlic. In a baking dish, alternate layers of vegetable sauce, cooked noodles and cheeses, ending with a fine layer of parmesan. Bake at 375 F for about 30 minutes. Cool slightly before serving.

Spinach Stuffed Pasta Shells
(serves 7)

3 heads spinach chopped
2 cups chopped mushrooms
2 tablespoon olive oil
1 cup ricotta cheese
4 tablespoons grated parmesan cheese
Grated peel and juice of 1 lemon, about 3 tablespoons juice
6 ounces large pasta shells, about 20
1¾ cups prepared spaghetti sauce mixed with 2 tablespoons of Italian seasonings, 4 cloves crushed garlic and salt to taste.

In skillet, over high heat, steam fresh spinach until wilted in water. Remove and drain. In same skillet, sauté mushrooms and onions in olive oil 2-3 minutes. Add spinach, ricotta cheese, garlic, 4 tablespoons parmesan cheese and lemon peel; mix well. Set aside. Add lemon juice to large pot of boiling water. Add pasta shells and cook until tender 10-12 minutes. Drain. Rinse with cold water and drain again.

Preheat oven to 375 F. Spray a 12x8x2 inch baking dish with cooking spray. Pour 1 cup spaghetti sauce into baking dish. Spoon about 1½ tablespoons spinach mixture into each shell; arrange on sauce in baking dish. Spoon remaining ¾ cup spaghetti sauce over shells. Sprinkle remaining 1 teaspoon parmesan cheese over top of sauce and shells. Bake until heated, about 25 minutes.

Vegetable Pot Pie

Pastry Topping:
1⅔ cups whole wheat flour
½ teaspoon salt
½ teaspoon baking powder
1 stick (8 tablespoons) cold butter, cut into small pieces
4½ tablespoons ice-cold water

2 medium all-purpose potatoes, peeled and cut in ½ inch dice (2⅓ cups)
2 large carrots peeled and cut in to ⅓ inch pieces
1½ cups corn
1½ cups frozen baby peas
1½ tablespoons butter
1 large onion, finely chopped
1 rib celery, finely chopped (⅔ cup)
1 tablespoon virgin olive oil
¼ cup all-purpose flour
1½ cups vegetable broth
1 cup soy milk
1 teaspoon dried thyme
Salt to taste

Make pastry: in food processor, combine flour, butter, salt and baking powder and pulse on/off until mixture resembles fine crumbs. Add 3 tablespoons ice water. Pulse on/off until mixture is evenly dampened. Sprinkled with remaining 1¼ tablespoons water and process until dough forms large crumbs and can be easily packed.

Transfer dough to work surface and form into ball. Knead dough 2 or 3 times, then place on large sheet of plastic wrap. Flatten into ¾-inch thick disk. Wrap in plastic and refrigerate 1 hour.

Preheat oven to 400 F. Meanwhile, make filling. Bring medium pot of lightly salted water to a boil. Add potatoes and carrots,

(continued on next page)

boil 5 minutes then add corn and peas. Drain vegetables and transfer to medium bowl.

In medium saucepan, melt 1½ tablespoons butter over medium heat. Add onion and celery and cook, stirring often, until onion has softened (8-9 minutes). Stir in oil and flour and cook over low heat, stirring for 1 minute. Stir in vegetable broth. Increase heat to medium. Cook, stirring until mixture thickens (about 2 minutes). Stir in soy milk and cook, stirring constantly, until thickened (about 1½ minutes). Pour sauce over vegetables and stir to mix well. Season with thyme and salt to taste.

Transfer vegetables to 9½ or 10 inch deep dish pie pan; smooth top. Let cool for 15 minutes. On a sheet of lightly floured wax paper, roll pastry into circle just slightly larger than pie pan. Invert pastry over pie pan and peel off paper. Tuck edges of pastry inside edge of pan. Poke several stream vents in crust with knife. Bake until pastry is golden (50 to 60 minutes). Let stand briefly before serving.

Fried Scrambled Tofu (eggs)
(serves 4)

1 block of firm tofu
1 chopped green pepper
1 chopped onion
1 chopped tomato
2 tablespoons olive oil
Salt and pepper to taste

Squeeze moisture from tofu, crumble tofu. Heat olive oil in skillet. Scramble all ingredients together. Salt and pepper to taste.

Mexican Delight

1 large zucchini
1 green bell pepper
1 large carrot
½ cup cooked kidney beans
2 teaspoons olive oil
1 summer squash
1 cup corn
1 onion
1 teaspoon water
1 tablespoon olive oil

Dressing:
1-2 teaspoons olive oil
½ teaspoon ground red chili (not chili powder)
Juice of 1 lime
½ teaspoon sea salt

Cut zucchini, summer squash, bell peppers, carrot and onion into thick pieces of equal size. Set aside. Combine dressing ingredients in a jar or small bowl and set aside.

Heat oil in frying pan or wok until oil is very hot and just starting to smoke. Add all vegetables except corn and stir until all surfaces of vegetables are coated with oil and look cooked. Add corn and water and immediately cover. Let steam for about one minute. Uncover and add kidney beans. Cover and let cook for another minute. Turn off heat. Toss vegetables with dressing and serve.

Eggplant-Polenta Casserole
(serves 8-10)

---

2 tablespoons olive oil
1 medium eggplant (1-1¼ pounds) peeled and cut into 1-inch chunks
2 medium Portobello mushrooms, stemmed and cut into 1-inch chunks or use regular mushrooms
1 zucchini, cut into 1-inch chunks
1 yellow summer squash, cut into 1-inch chunks
4 medium cloves of garlic, smashed
25 ounce jar of pasta sauce, mixed with 3 tablespoons Italian seasonings
15 ounce can of white beans, rinsed and drained or cook your own.
24 ounce prepared polenta roll, sliced (about ½ inch thick)
8 ounces soy mozzarella shredded (2 cups)
Salt to taste

In large, deep nonstick skillet, heat oil over medium heat. Add eggplant and mushrooms; cook, stirring often, until eggplant has softened (about 8 minutes). Add zucchini, squash and garlic and cook until squash is just tender (about 6 minutes). Stir in pasta sauce, beans and salt. Reduce heat to low and simmer for 30 minutes, stirring occasionally. Add garlic.

Preheat oven to 350 F. With vegetable cooking spray, coat a 13x9 inch baking dish. Arrange polenta in bottom of dish, and then sprinkle with half of the shredded cheese. Spoon sauce mixture on top and sprinkle with smashed garlic. Sprinkle with remaining cheese. Bake until bubbly (about 20 minutes). Let cool of 10-15 minutes before cutting.

Sweet Potato Casserole
(serves 6-8)

1 cinnamon stick
1 cup water
4 pounds of yams or sweet potatoes, peeled and sliced
   ½ inch thick
½ cup firmly packed light brown sugar
4 tablespoons butter

Place all ingredients in sauce pan and cover. Cook over medium heat until potatoes are soft (about 20-30 minutes). Stir several times with wooden spoon to mix, being careful not to break the potatoes. Remove cinnamon stick.

Remove cover from yams or sweet potatoes when tender, and continue cooking until water is almost evaporated and liquid is syrupy. Remove from heat and transfer to serving bowl and serve hot.

Vegetable Hearty Stew

1 tablespoon olive oil
1 large onion, sliced
4 clove garlic, chopped
1 jalapeño pepper, seeded and minced (optional)
1 pound medium sized yellow summer squash,
  cut into ¾ inch thick slices
2 medium sized zucchini, cut into 1 inch chunks
1 pound of green beans, cut into 1 inch pieces
1 cup corn kernels, preferably fresh
2 16 ounce cans of kidney beans, drained and rinsed or
  cook your own
1 cup vegetable or chicken broth
1 tablespoon thyme
Salt and freshly ground pepper to taste

Heat the oil in a large stockpot or Dutch oven over medium heat. Add the onion and jalapeño pepper, and sauté until the onion is tender and translucent, about five minutes.

Stir in the remaining ingredients except the thyme, salt and pepper, and bring to a boil.

Reduce heat to low, and cook, covered, over low heat for 15-25 minutes, or until vegetables are tender. Add the thyme during the last 5 minutes of cooking. Add the salt, pepper and garlic, stirring them in well, and serve the stew warm.

Sesame Tofu with Vegetable Rice
(serves 4)

2 cups raw brown rice
7 cups vegetable stock
1 medium sized carrot, peeled and cut into 1-inch lengths
½ head broccoli, cut into florets
½ head cauliflower, cut into florets
2 scallions, thinly sliced
Salt and freshly ground pepper to taste

Tofu
1½ 15-ounce packages of extra firm tofu
1 cup tahini paste
½ cup Bragg's liquid aminos or soy sauce
½ cup honey
1½ cups vegetable stock
½ teaspoon chopped garlic
1 tablespoon lemon juice
½ teaspoon salt
2 scallions, sliced, as garnish

To make rice: place rice in stockpot and bring to a boil over high heat. Reduce heat to low, cover and cook for 20 minutes. Add carrots, broccoli, cauliflower and scallions, and continue to cook until all liquid is absorbed and cooked completely. Season with salt and pepper to taste.

To make tofu: slice tofu lengthwise in three sections, and cut each section in half. Combine tahini paste, liquid aminos, honey, stock, garlic, lemon juice, salt and ginger in food processor, and process until smooth.

Spray nonstick skillet with nonstick cooking spray, and heat over medium high heat. Place tofu in skillet, and sear both sides until golden. Pour sauce over tofu, reduce heat to low and cook until sauce is heated through (about 10 minutes). To serve, place sesame tofu and rice on plate, and garnish with scallions.

Barley-Zucchini Sauté

(serves 6)

---

1 cup raw barley
2 tablespoons vegetable oil
2 tablespoon minced garlic
3 medium sized leeks (¾ pound) rinsed and trimmed, white parts only
2 zucchini, rinsed, quartered and thinly sliced
4 ounces crumbled feta cheese
Salt and pepper to taste
2 tablespoons Spike

Cook barley according to package directions.

Heat oil in large skillet over medium heat and sauté leeks and zucchini about 8 minutes, or until leeks wilt and zucchini softens and turns golden.

When barley is cooked, spoon into skillet, and sauté with leeks and zucchini for about two minutes. Mix in garlic and seasonings.

Remove from heat, spoon onto individual plates and garnish with crumbled feta cheese. Serve hot or at room temperature.

Zucchini Pie
(6-8 servings)

---

4 cups thinly sliced zucchini
1 cup chopped onions
½ cup butter
½ cup chopped fresh parsley or 2 tablespoons dried parsley
Salt & pepper to taste
1 teaspoon garlic salt
1 teaspoon dried basil
1 teaspoon dried oregano
2 egg substitutes, beaten
2 cups of grated cheddar or Jack cheese
Dijon mustard
Deep dish whole wheat pie crust, frozen or homemade, thawed

Preheat oven to 375 F.

In a large skillet sauté the zucchini and onions in the butter for about 10 minutes. Add the spices and stir well. Set aside.

In large bowl combine the eggs and cheese, mix well. Add the zucchini mixture to the bowl and stir till well blended.

Use Dijon mustard to paint the inside of crust and then fill with zucchini mixture and bake for 18-20 minutes. Allow to stand for 10 minutes before serving.

Fresh Vegetable Pie
(6-8 servings)

2 tablespoons vegetable oil
2 garlic cloves, minced
1 medium chopped onion
3 medium chopped tomatoes
1 small eggplant, peeled and cubed
1 green pepper, chopped
1 cup corn
2 medium zucchini, sliced
6 tablespoons grated parmesan cheese
1 unbaked 9 inch whole wheat pie shell, frozen or homemade
2 tablespoons butter
Salt and pepper to taste

Preheat oven to 350 F.

Heat oil in large skillet on medium high heat. Add the tomatoes, onion, eggplant and green pepper. Sauté about 7 minutes, until vegetables begin to get tender. Add the zucchini and continue cooking until it is almost tender. Remove from heat. Mix in garlic. Sprinkle 2 tablespoons of the cheese over unbaked pie crust. Add half the vegetables using a slotted spoon to avoid getting extra liquid from the vegetables into the pie. Sprinkle 2 tablespoons cheese and 1 tablespoon butter. Add the remaining vegetables, top with the rest of butter. Bake for about 40 minutes, until the crust is golden brown.

Tortellini with Roasted Vegetable Sauce

2 tablespoon Italian seasoning
½ pound chopped mushrooms
1 package of Ricotta & Spinach Tortellini
1 medium zucchini, cut into 1 inch pieces
1 medium yellow squash, cut into 1 inch pieces
1 small eggplant, cut into 1 inch pieces
1 large onion, slices
3 plum tomatoes, halved lengthwise
1 cup Italian salad dressing
Salt and pepper to taste

Marinate vegetables in salad dressing for 15 minutes. Mix with seasonings and place in a broiler pan. Grill vegetables under broiler until browned, approximately 7 minutes per side. In the meantime, cook the Tortellini according to package directions. Heat remaining salad dressing and pour over drained tortellini and vegetables. Toss gently and serve.

Eggplant Sandwiches with Pepper Yogurt Sauce
(serves 6)

Pepper-Yogurt Sauce:
1 cup nonfat plain soy yogurt
½ cup light mayonnaise
⅓ cup packed fresh basil leaves, thinly sliced
3 cloves garlic, smashed
Olive oil
Salt and pepper to taste

Sandwiches:
1 firm medium-sized eggplant (about ¾ of a pound), cut into ½ inch thick slices
Garlic salt to taste
2 cups lettuce, washed, dried
1 teaspoon olive oil
6 whole wheat pita pockets
1 sliced bell pepper

To make Pepper Yogurt Sauce:
Whisk yogurt, mayonnaise, basil and garlic with oil to blend in medium bowl. Season to taste with salt and pepper. Cover and refrigerate until ready to use.

To make Sandwiches:
Preheat broiler. Brush eggplant and bell pepper with olive oil and garlic salt. On rack of broiler pan, arrange eggplant slices in one layer. Broil eggplant about 4 inches from heat, until golden, turning once, 3-5 minutes on each side. Spread pita pockets on one side with pepper-yogurt sauce. Fill each pita with eggplant, pepper, lettuce and top with more yogurt sauce if desired.

White Bean Casserole
(serves 4)

1 tablespoon olive oil
4 small shallots, quartered
4 cloves of garlic, minced
3 carrots, peeled and sliced into 1/4 inch rounds
1 turnip, peeled and chopped
1 parsnip, peeled and sliced into 1/4 inch rounds
1 14.5 ounce can crushed tomatoes, undrained
1½ cups vegetable stock or water
2 bay leaves, crushed
1¼ teaspoon dried thyme or savory
2 cups great northern beans, cooked according to directions on package
Salt and pepper to taste

Heat oil in 5-6 quart Dutch oven or other large pot over medium heat. Add shallots and carrots. Cover and cook for 5 minutes to soften. Reduce heat to low and add remaining ingredients except beans. Cook, stirring occasionally, until vegetables are tender, about 15 minutes. Mix in garlic, salt, pepper and beans. Serve.

Fiesta Tamale Pie
(serves 6)

2 tablespoons salad oil
1 medium onion, chopped
4 garlic cloves, minced
1 pound of soy hamburger
½ pound soy sausage
1 28 ounce can tomatoes
1 16 ounce can corn, drained
1 tablespoon chili powder
2 tablespoons Mexican seasoning
½ teaspoon oregano leaves
½ teaspoon ground cumin
1 cup pitted ripe olives, drained
2 egg substitutes, lightly beaten
1 cup soy milk
1 cup cornmeal
1½ cups shredded cheddar cheese

Preheat oven to 350 F. Heat oil in frying pan over medium heat. Add onion and cook until onion is soft. Crumble soy hamburger and sausage into pan and cook until well browned. Stir in tomatoes (break with a spoon) and their excess liquid, corn, chili powder, oregano and cumin. Cover, reduce heat, and simmer for 10 minutes. Stir in olives and garlic. Spread in a shallow 3-quart casserole dish or 9x13 inch baking pan.

In bowl, combine eggs and milk, then stir in cornmeal; spoon over soy mixture, making sure cornmeal is well distributed. Sprinkle with cheese. Bake, uncovered, for 45 minutes, or until top is lightly set and browned.

Millan's Mother's Famous Stuffed Bell Peppers
(serves 4)

◆

4 slightly cooked bell peppers, tops removed and insides scooped out
1 medium chopped onion
2 chopped tomatoes
4 chopped celery ribs
3 cups cooked wild brown rice cooked with 1 vegetable bouillon cube
1 teaspoon cumin
2 tablespoons Spike seasoning
2 bay leaves, crushed
1 heaping tablespoon basil
1 heaping tablespoon Mrs. Dash
Salt to taste
4 slices of cheddar cheese (small enough to place on the bottom of a bell pepper)

Sauté vegetables in 2 tablespoons olive oil. Add cumin, bay leaves, basil, Mrs. Dash, and salt to taste. Mix together with rice. Place small slice of cheddar cheese on bottom of each bell pepper cover and stuff peppers with vegetable and rice mix. Bake for 10-15 minutes.

Family Favorite Fideo
from Lupe Campos, my precious stepmother
(serves 4)

---

1 can chicken broth
1 large onion, chopped
3 large tomatoes, chopped
2 tablespoons Mexican seasoning
Salt to taste
4 cloves crushed garlic
1 package of fideo
2 tablespoons olive oil
3 tablespoons parmesan cheese

Fry onion in oil until softened. Add tomatoes and seasoning and continue to fry with 1 cup chicken broth. Remove from skillet. In clean skillet, add 1 tablespoon oil and fry fideo until brown on both sides. Be careful not to burn fideo. Add tomatoes, garlic and onion mixture and simmer on low for 10 minutes or until it is cooked. Sprinkle top with parmesan cheese.

Portobello Pizzettas
(serves 6)

Preheat oven to 350 F.
4 cups fresh spinach, cleaned and finely chopped
1½ cups mozzarella cheese, shredded
¾ cup finely chopped veggie pepperoni
¼ teaspoon ground pepper
12 fresh Portobello mushrooms, 3-4 inch diameter
2 tablespoons dried basil
2 tablespoons Italian seasonings
Salt to taste

Combine all ingredients except mushrooms. Mix well. Clean mushrooms; remove stems and place open side up on cookie sheet. Spray each mushroom lightly with olive oil. Spoon 2 tablespoons of spinach mixture on top. Bake 12 minutes. Garnish with fresh basil.

Vegetable Fiesta Casserole
(serves 8)

Preheat oven to 350 F.
1 cup chopped carrots
1 cup chopped onion
1 small zucchini, chopped
1 15 ounce can kidney beans, drained and rinsed or cook your own
2 cups corn
1 small green pepper, chopped
1 15 ounce can tomato sauce
2 cups medium-hot low or no sodium salsa
¼ cup water
4 teaspoon taco seasoning
1 cup shredded non-fat or low-fat veggie cheese (soy, rice or almond) or cheddar cheese
Salt to taste

Spray large nonstick skillet with cooking spray. Heat over medium-high heat until hot. Add carrots, green pepper, zucchini and onion. Cook, stirring, 8-10 minutes or until vegetables are tender, add salt and 2 to 3 tablespoons water if necessary to prevent sticking.

Stir in remaining ingredients except cheese and heat. Sprinkle with cheese. Cover; let stand until cheese is melted.

Heavenly Shepherd Pie
(serves 8)

Filling:
1 cup vegetable or chicken broth
3 cloves garlic, minced
2 medium onions, finely chopped
1 large green pepper, diced
2 medium carrots, thinly sliced
2 large ribs celery, chopped
2 cups sliced mushrooms
1 15 ounce can diced tomatoes
1 15 ounce can kidney beans, drained and rinsed or
    cook your own
2½ cups of ground soy burger granules
3 tablespoons whole wheat flour
½ teaspoon oregano
½ teaspoon tarragon
½ teaspoon thyme
½ teaspoon basil
½ teaspoon black pepper
1 teaspoon freshly chopped parsley
2 tablespoon Bragg's liquid aminos
Salt to taste

Mashed Potato Topping:
5 large potatoes, thinly sliced
½ cup to 1 cup soy cream
Salt to taste
Pepper to taste
1 teaspoon paprika

In a large pot, heat stock. Add onions green pepper, carrots and celery. Cook over medium heat 8-10 minutes. Add mushrooms, liquid aminos, tomatoes and kidney beans. Cover and cook 10 minutes. Add soy burger granules, flour and spices. Cook 5 minutes, stirring constantly. Add garlic then pour into a 9x13 inch pan, lightly sprayed with olive oil. Set aside.

(continued on next page)

Steam potatoes until tender and mash in enough soy cream to make them smooth and spreadable. Add salt and pepper to taste. Spread mashed potatoes evenly over the top of the veggie mixture. Sprinkle with paprika. Bake 20 minutes until hot and bubbly.

Cabbage and Walnut Stir-Fry
(serves 4)

12 ounce white cabbage
12 ounce red cabbage
4 tablespoons oil
2 garlic cloves, crushed
8 scallions
Package firm tofu, liquid squeezed out and cubed
2 tablespoons lemon juice
3½ ounces walnut halves
2 teaspoon Dijon mustard
2 teaspoon poppy seeds
Salt and pepper to taste
Liquid aminos to taste

Using a sharp knife, shred the white and red cabbages thinly and set aside until required.

Heat the oil in a preheated wok or heavy-bottomed skillet. Add the cabbage, scallions and tofu and cook, stirring constantly, for 5 minutes. Add liquid aminos.

Add the lemon juice, walnuts, and Dijon mustard, season to taste with salt and pepper and cook for another 5 minutes, or until the cabbage is tender. Add garlic.

Transfer the stir-fry to a warm serving bowl, sprinkle with poppy seeds and serve immediately with brown rice.

Stuffed Egg Plant
(serves 4)

---

2 medium eggplants, halved lengthwise
Salt to taste
4 tablespoons olive oil
2 large onions, sliced thinly
2 garlic cloves, crushed
1 green pepper, sliced
1 14 ounce can chopped tomatoes
1½ ounces brown sugar
1 teaspoon ground coriander
Ground black pepper
2 tablespoons fresh coriander or parsley, chopped

Using a sharp knife, slash the flesh of the eggplants a few times. Sprinkle with salt and place in a colander for about half an hour. Rinse well and pat dry.

Gently fry the eggplants, cut side down, in the oil for 5 minutes, then drain and place in a shallow ovenproof dish.

In the same pan gently fry the onions, and green pepper, adding extra oil if necessary. Cook for about 10 minutes, or until vegetables have softened.

Add the tomatoes, sugar, ground coriander and seasoning and cook for about 5 minutes until the mixture is reduced. Stir in the chopped coriander or parsley and garlic.

Spoon this mixture on top of the eggplants. Preheat the oven to 375 F, cover and bake for about 30-35 minutes. When cooked, cool, then chill. Serve cold with crusty bread.

Potato and Cabbage Croquettes
(serves 4)

1 pound/3 cups mashed potatoes
8 ounce steamed or boiled cabbage or kale, shredded
1 egg substitute, beaten
4 ounce cheddar cheese, grated
Nutmeg
Salt and ground pepper to taste
All-purpose flour, for coating
Oil, for frying

Mix the potatoes with the cabbage or kale, egg, cheese, nutmeg, and seasoning. Divide and shape into eight croquettes.

Chill for an hour or so, if possible, as this enables the mixture to become firm and makes it easier to fry. Toss the croquettes in the flour. Heat about ½ inch of oil in a frying pan until it is quite hot.

Carefully slide the croquettes into the oil and fry on each side for about 3 minutes until golden and crisp. Drain on paper towel and serve hot and crisp.

Tofu and Vegetables
(serves 4)

---

2 8 ounce cartons smoked tofu, cubed
3 tablespoons Bragg's liquid aminos
2 tablespoons dry sherry or vermouth
4 tablespoons virgin olive oil
2 leeks, thinly sliced
2 carrots, cut in sticks
1 large zucchini, thinly sliced
1 can baby corn halved
4 ounces button or shiitake mushrooms, sliced
1 tablespoon sesame seeds
1 package of egg noodles, preferably wheat, cooked

Marinate the tofu in the liquid aminos, sherry or vermouth and sesame oil for at least half an hour. Drain and reserve the marinade.

Heat the oil in a wok and stir-fry the tofu cubes until browned all over. Remove and reserve.

Stir-fry the leeks, carrots, zucchini and baby corn, stirring and tossing for about 10 minutes. Add the mushrooms and cook for a further minute.

Return the tofu to the wok with the vegetables and pour in the marinade. Heat until bubbling, then scatter over the sesame seeds.

Serve as soon as possible with the hot cooked noodles, dressed in a little sesame oil, if desired.

Pita Pizzas
(serves 4)

Extra toppings-choose from:
1 small red onion, thinly sliced and lightly fried
Mushrooms, sliced and fried
1 7 ounce can corn, drained
Jalapeño peppers, sliced optional
Black or green olives, pitted and sliced
Capers, drained

Basic Pizzas:
4 pita breads, ideally whole wheat
Small jar of pasta sauce mix with 4 cloves crushed garlic and
    2 tablespoon Italian seasonings
8 ounces mozzarella cheese, sliced or grated
Dried oregano or thyme, to sprinkle
Salt and ground black pepper to taste

Prepare two or three toppings of your choice for the pizzas.

Preheat the broiler and lightly toast the pita breads on each side.

Spread pasta sauce on each pita, right to the edge. This prevents the edges of the pita from burning.

Arrange cheese slices or grated cheese on top of each pita and sprinkle with herbs and seasoning.

Add the toppings of your choice and then broil the pizzas for about 5-8 minutes until they are golden brown and bubbling. Serve immediately.

Pepper and Potato Tortilla from Spain

(serves 4)

2 medium sized potatoes sliced
3 tablespoons olive oil
1 large onion, chopped
2 garlic cloves, crushed
2 peppers, one green and one red, chopped
5 egg whites or egg substitute, beaten slightly
2 tablespoons of Spike seasonings
Salt and ground black pepper to taste

Heat the oil and fry the potatoes till tender. Add the onion and peppers cooking over a moderate heat for 5 minutes until softened. Add more oil if needed.

Pour in the eggs, mixed with seasonings and garlic.

Continue to cook on a low heat, without stirring, half covering the pan with a lid to help set the eggs.

When the mixture is firm, flash the pan under the hot broiler to seal the top just lightly. Leave the tortilla in the pan to cool. This helps it to firm up further and makes it easier to turn out.

Cauliflower Casserole
(serves 4)

1 medium-sized cauliflower, broken in florets
1 medium onion, chopped
2 eggs, hard boiled, peeled and chopped
3 tablespoons whole wheat flour
1 teaspoon mild curry powder
2 tablespoons butter
2 cups soy milk
1 teaspoon dried thyme
Salt and ground black pepper to taste
4 ounce sharp cheese, grated

Boil the cauliflower and onion in enough salted water to cover until they are just tender. Be careful not to overcook them. Drain well.

Arrange the cauliflower and onion in a shallow, ovenproof dish and scatter over the chopped egg.

Put the flour, curry powder, butter and milk in a saucepan all together. Bring slowly to a boil, stirring well until thickened and smooth. Stir in the thyme and seasoning and allow the sauce to simmer for a minute or two. Remove the pan from the heat and stir in about three quarters of the cheese.

Pour the sauce over the cauliflower, and sprinkle with the remaining cheese. Brown under a hot broiler until golden and serve.

Broccoli Casserole
(serves 8)

---

2 tablespoons butter
2 pounds broccoli, chopped
1 large onion, chopped
2 large egg substitutes or 3 egg whites
1 can (10¾ ounces) cream of celery soup
1 cup shredded sharp cheese
¼ cup mayonnaise
Cooking oil spray
½ cup bread crumbs

Preheat oven to 350 F. Melt the butter by placing it in a cup glass measure. Cover with a paper towel, and cook in the microwave for 30-45 seconds on high until mostly melted. Remove from the microwave and stir until completely melted. Set aside.

In a large bowl, lightly beat eggs. Add melted butter, onion, mayonnaise, celery soup and cheese. Mix well, then add broccoli. Stir well until broccoli is coated with sauce. (May be covered and refrigerated up to 8 hours at this point.)

Spray a 13x9 inch casserole dish with cooking oil spray. Pour the broccoli mixture into the dish, and smooth with the back of a spoon. (The casserole may be frozen for up to a month at this point. Allow the casserole to thaw for 24 hours in the refrigerator and set out while you preheat the oven. Then proceed to the next step.)

Bake in the middle of the oven, uncovered, until the top begins to brown. Sprinkle the crumbs evenly on top and continue to bake, uncovered, until the crumbs brown, about 10 minutes.

Cheesy, Zucchini Rice Bake

1 small jalapeño, seeded and finely chopped (optional)
1 yellow onion, diced
1 red pepper, diced
3 cups cooked brown rice
3 cups chopped zucchini, small bite sized
Salt to taste
1 teaspoon paprika
1 teaspoon dried basil
1½ cups shredded Swiss cheese
4 tablespoons olive oil, divided

Preheat oven to 350 F.

Sauté zucchini in 2 tablespoons olive oil until just tender, add salt and put to the side. With remaining oil sauté jalapeño, onion, pepper, paprika, and basil until onion begins to turn clear and pepper softens. In covered casserole dish combine all ingredients including rice and ¼ cup of Swiss cheese. Top casserole with remaining ¼ cup of cheese, cover and bake for 15 minutes.

Vegetarian Chili

(10 1-cup servings)

Nonstick vegetable oil cooking spray
2 teaspoons olive oil
2 cups chopped onion
2 cups chopped green bell pepper
4 medium cloves of garlic, minced
2 cups chicken broth
1 cup canned diced tomatoes
1 cup bulgur wheat
2 tablespoons ground cumin
2 tablespoons Mexican seasoning
1½ tablespoons chili powder or to taste
1 tablespoon lemon juice
½ teaspoon cayenne
2 cans (16 ounces each) kidney beans, rinsed and drained, or cook your own
Salt to taste

Heat a large saucepan or Dutch oven over medium high heat.

Add the oil. Sauté the onions and bell peppers for 8-10 minutes, or until the bell peppers are tender, stirring frequently. Reduce the heat if necessary to prevent burning.

Stir in the chicken broth, tomatoes, bulgur, all seasonings and lemon juice. Reduce the heat and simmer, covered, for 30 minutes or until the bulgur is done and the flavors are blended. Stir in the beans, garlic and salt. Heat uncovered. Serve.

Asparagus Stir Fry

2 cloves minced garlic
1 pound asparagus, chopped
2 carrots sliced thin
½ pound mushrooms sliced
3 tablespoons oil
2 tablespoons sesame seeds

Sauté vegetables in wok till tender.

Sauce:
½ tablespoon ginger powder
2 teaspoons cornstarch
½ cup chicken broth
Bragg's liquid aminos to taste

Mix in blender. Heat till thickens. Pour over vegetables.

Potatoes with Blue Cheese and Walnuts
(serves 4)

1 pound small new potatoes cut in quarters
2 ribs of celery, sliced
Small red onion, sliced
4 ounces blue cheese, mashed
⅔ cup soy cream
Salt and ground black pepper to taste
1 cup walnuts, chopped
2 tablespoons Spike seasoning
2 tablespoons fresh parsley, chopped

Cover the potatoes with water and boil till slightly tender, adding the sliced celery and onion to the pan for the last 5 minutes or so.

Drain the vegetables and put them into a shallow serving dish.

In a small saucepan melt the cheese in the cream slowly, stirring occasionally. Do not allow the mixture to boil but heat it until it scalds.

Season the sauce to taste. Add Spike. Pour it over the vegetables and garnish with walnuts and parsley. Serve hot.

Falafel

(makes 8)

1 15 ounce can chick peas, drained or cook your own
2 garlic cloves, crushed
2 tablespoons fresh parsley, chopped
2 tablespoons coriander
1 teaspoon fresh mint, chopped
1 teaspoon cumin
2 tablespoons fresh breadcrumbs
1 teaspoon salt
Ground black pepper
Oil, for deep frying

Grind the chick peas in a food processor until they are just smooth, then mix them with all the other ingredients until you have a thick, creamy paste. Add pepper to taste.

Using wet hands, shape the chick pea mixture into 8 balls and chill for 30 minutes so that they become firm.

Meanwhile, heat about ¼ inch of oil in a shallow frying pan and fry the balls a few at a time. Cook each one for about 8 minutes, turning them all carefully just once.

Drain each ball on a paper towel and fry the rest in batches, reheating the oil in between. Serve tucked inside warm pita breads with sliced salad, tomatoes and tahini cream or yogurt.

Magnificent Zucchini
(serves 4-6)

3 cups whole wheat pasta shells
3-4 pounds zucchini
1 onion, chopped
1 pepper, seeded and chopped
1 tablespoon fresh ginger root, grated
4 garlic cloves, crushed
3 teaspoons oil
4 large tomatoes, skinned and chopped
Salt and ground black pepper to taste
½ cup pine nuts
2 tablespoons basil
Cheese, grated, to serve (optional)

Preheat the oven to 375 F. Boil the pasta according to the instructions on the package. Drain thoroughly and set to one side.

Cut the zucchini in half lengthwise. Use a small sharp knife and tablespoon to scoop out the zucchini flesh. Chop the flesh roughly.

Gently fry the onion, pepper, ginger and garlic in the oil for 5 minutes then add the zucchini flesh, tomatoes and seasoning. Cover and cook for 10-12 minutes until the vegetables are soft.

Add to the pan the pasta, pine nuts and basil, stir well and set aside.

Meanwhile, place the zucchini halves in a roasting pan, season lightly and pour a little water around the zucchini, taking care it does not spill inside. Cover with foil and bake for 15 minutes.

Remove the foil, discard the water and fill the shells with the vegetable mixture. Re-cover with foil and return to the oven for a further 10 minutes.

If you wish, serve this dish topped with grated cheese. The zucchini can either be served cut into sections or scooped out of the "shell."

Favorite Spinach with Filo
(serves 8)

———◆———

10 ounces fresh leaf spinach, well washed
2 scallions, chopped
6 ounces feta cheese, crumbled
2 egg whites slightly beaten
1 tablespoon fresh dill, chopped
Salt and pepper to taste
4 large sheets or 8 small sheets of filo pastry
Olive oil, for brushing

Preheat the oven to 375 F. Blanch the spinach in the tiniest amount of water until just wilted, then drain very well, pressing it through a sieve with the back of a wooden spoon.

Chop the spinach finely and mix with the scallions, feta, egg, dill, salt and pepper.

Lay out a sheet of filo pastry and brush with olive oil. If large, cut the pieces in two and sandwich them together. If small, fit another sheet on top and brush with olive oil.

Spread a quarter of the filling on one edge of the filo at the bottom, then roll it up firmly, but not too tightly. Shape into a crescent and place on a baking sheet.

Brush the pastry well with oil and bake for about 20-25 minutes in the preheated oven until golden and crisp. Cool slightly then remove to a wire rack to cool further.

Chunky Vegetable Paella
(serves 6)

Good pinch saffron strands
1 eggplant, cut in thick chunks
Salt to taste
6 tablespoons olive oil
1 large onion, sliced
4 garlic cloves, crushed
1 yellow pepper, sliced
1 red pepper, sliced
2 teaspoons paprika
1¼ cups Arborio rice
2½ cups vegetable or chicken broth
1 pound fresh tomatoes, skinned and chopped
Salt and pepper to taste
4 ounces sliced mushrooms
4 ounces cut green beans
1 15 ounce can chick peas or cook your own
1½ cups baby peas

Steep the saffron in 3 tablespoons hot water. Sprinkle the eggplant with salt, leave to drain in a colander for 30 minutes, then rinse and dry.

In a large frying pan, heat the oil and fry the onion, peppers and eggplant for about 5 minutes, stirring occasionally. Sprinkle in the paprika and stir again.

Mix in the rice, then pour in the stock, tomatoes, saffron and seasoning. Bring to a boil then simmer for 15 minutes, uncovered, shaking the pan frequently and stirring occasionally.

Stir in the mushrooms, green beans, baby peas and chick peas (with the liquid). Continue cooking for another 10 minutes, then add garlic and serve hot from the pan.

Tangy Fricassè
(serves 4)

◆

4 zucchini, sliced
4 ounces green beans, sliced
4 large tomatoes, skinned and sliced
1 onion, sliced
4 tablespoons butter
⅓ cup whole wheat flour
2 teaspoons coarse grain mustard
2 cups soy milk
⅔ cup plain soy yogurt
1 teaspoon dried thyme
4 ounces sharp cheese, grated
Salt and ground black pepper to taste
4 tablespoons fresh whole wheat bread crumbs tossed with
　　1 tablespoon oil

Blanch the zucchini and beans in a small amount of boiling water for just 5 minutes, then drain and arrange in a shallow, ovenproof dish.

Arrange all but three sliced of tomato on top. Put the onion into a saucepan with the butter or margarine and fry gently for 5 minutes.

Stir in the flour and mustard, cook for a minute then add the soy milk gradually until the sauce has thickened. Simmer for another 2 minutes.

Remove the pan from the heat, add the yogurt, thyme and cheese, stirring until melted. Season to taste. Reheat gently if you wish, but do not allow the sauce to boil or it will curdle.

Pour the sauce over the vegetables and scatter the breadcrumbs on top. Brown under a preheated broiler until golden and crisp, taking care not to let them burn. Garnish with the reserved tomato slices if desired.

Curried Parsnip Pie
(serves 4)

─────◆─────

Pastry:
½ cup butter
1 cup whole wheat flour
Salt and ground black pepper to taste
1 teaspoon dried thyme or oregano
Cold water, to mix

Filling:
8 baby onions, or shallots, peeled
2 large parsnips, thinly sliced
2 carrots, thinly sliced
2 tablespoons butter
2 tablespoons whole wheat flour
1 tablespoon curry
1¼ cups soy cream
4 ounces sharp cheese, grated
Salt and ground black pepper to taste
3 tablespoons coriander or parsley, chopped

Make the pastry by rubbing the butter into the flour until it resembles fine breadcrumbs. Season and stir in the thyme or oregano, then mix to a firm dough with cold water.

Blanch the baby onions or shallots with the parsnips and carrots in just enough water to cover, for about 5 minutes. Drain, reserving about 1¼ cups of the liquid.

In a clean pan, melt the butter and stir in the flour to make a roux. Gradually whisk in the reserved stock and soy cream until smooth. Simmer for a minute or two.

Take the pan off the heat, stir in the cheese and seasoning, then mix into the vegetables with the coriander or parsley.

Pour into a pie dish.

Roll out the pastry, large enough to fit the top of the pie dish and trim edges. Make 2 slits on top of pie crust.

Place the pie on a baking sheet and chill for 30 minutes while you preheat the oven to 400 F. Bake the pie for about 25-30 minutes until golden brown and crisp on top.

Stuffed Potato and Parsnip
(serves 4)

4 large baking potatoes
Olive oil, for greasing
8 ounces parsnips, diced
2 tablespoons butter
1 teaspoon cumin seeds
1 teaspoon ground coriander
2 tablespoons soy cream or soy yogurt
Salt and ground black pepper to taste
4 ounces cheddar cheese, grated
2 egg whites, slightly beaten
¼ cup slivered almonds

Rub the potatoes all over with oil, score in half, then bake at 400 F for about 1 hour until cooked.

Meanwhile, boil the parsnips until tender, then drain well. Mash and mix with the butter, spices and cream or yogurt.

When the potatoes are cooked, halve, scoop out and mash the flesh then mix with the parsnip, seasoning well.

Stir in the cheese, egg and three quarters of the almonds. Fill the potato shells with the mixture and sprinkle over the remaining almonds.

Return to the oven and bake for about 15-20 minutes until golden brown and the filling has set lightly. Serve hot with a side salad.

Jeff's Favorite Stuffed Cabbage Rolls

(serves 4-6)

---

12 large cabbage or Swiss chard leaves, stalks removed
Salt to taste
2 tablespoons virgin olive oil
1 onion, chopped
2 large carrots, grated
8 ounces sliced mushrooms
2 cups vegetable or chicken broth
½ cup long grain brown rice
4 tablespoons lentils, cooked
1 teaspoon dried oregano or marjoram
Salt and pepper to taste

Blanch the leaves in boiling, salted water until they begin to wilt. Drain, reserve the water and pat the leaves dry with a paper towel.

Heat the oil and lightly fry the onion, carrots and mushrooms for 5 minutes, and then pour in the broth. Cook rice according to directions.

Add the lentils, rice, herbs and seasoning, and mix well. Remove from the heat, then stir in the cheese. Preheat the oven to 375 F.

Lay out the chard or cabbage leaves rib side down, and spoon on the filling at the stalk end. Fold the sides in and roll up.

Place the joint side down in a small roasting pan and pour in the reserved cabbage water. Cover with lightly greased foil and bake for 30-45 minutes until the leaves are tender. Sprinkle top with a little parmesan cheese.

Potato and Parsnip Delish
(serves 4-6)

2 pounds potatoes, thinly sliced
1 onion, thinly sliced
1 pound parsnips, thinly sliced
4 garlic cloves, crushed
4 tablespoons butter
4 ounces cheddar cheese, grated
¼ teaspoon nutmeg
Salt and ground black pepper to taste
1¼ cups soy cream
1¼ cups soy milk

Lightly grease a large, shallow, ovenproof dish and then preheat the oven to 350 F.

Layer the potatoes with the onion and the parsnips. In between each layer, dot the vegetables with garlic and butter, sprinkle over most of the cheese, add the nutmeg and season well.

Heat the cream and soy milk together in a saucepan until they are hot but not boiling. Slowly pour the creamy milk over the vegetables, making sure it seeps underneath them.

Scatter the remaining cheese over the vegetables and sprinkle a little more nutmeg on top. Bake for about an hour or so until the potatoes are tender and the cheese top is bubbling and golden.

Pasta and Mushroom Casserole
(serves 4-6)

7 ounces whole wheat pasta, small shapes
2½ cups soy milk
1 bay leaf crushed
Small onion stuck with 6 whole cloves
4 tablespoons butter
3 tablespoons fresh bread crumbs
2 tablespoons dried mixed herbs
⅓ cup whole wheat flour
4 tablespoons parmesan cheese
Sprinkle of nutmeg
Salt and ground black pepper to taste
2 egg substitute, or 3 egg whites slightly beaten
16 ounce button mushrooms, sliced
4 garlic cloves, crushed
2 tablespoons olive oil
2 tablespoons fresh parsley, chopped

Boil the pasta according to the instructions on the package. Drain and set aside. Heat the soy milk with the bay leaf and clove-studded onion and let stand for 15 minutes. Remove the onion.

Melt the butter in a saucepan and use a little to brush the inside of a large oval casserole dish. Mix the crumbs and mixed herbs together and use them to coat the inside of the dish.

Stir the flour into the butter, cook for a minute then slowly add the hot milk to make a smooth sauce. Add the cheese, nutmeg, seasoning and cooked pasta. Cool for 5 minutes then add the eggs.

Fry the button mushrooms in the oil for 3 minutes. Season, stir in the liquid and reduce down. Add the parsley and garlic.

Spoon a layer of pasta into the dish. Sprinkle over the mushrooms then more pasta and so on, finishing with pasta. Cover with greased foil. Heat the oven to 375 F and bake for about 25-30 minutes. Allow to stand 5 minutes before turning out to serve.

Eggplant Boats
(serves 4)

⅔ cups brown rice
2 medium-sized eggplants, halved lengthwise
1 onion, chopped
4 garlic cloves, crushed
1 green pepper, chopped
6 ounces mushrooms, sliced
3 tablespoons olive oil
3 ounces cheddar cheese, grated
1 egg substitute or 2 egg whites slightly beaten
1 teaspoon marjoram
Salt and ground black pepper
2 tablespoons hazelnuts, chopped

Boil the rice according to the instructions on the package, drain and then cool. Scoop out the flesh from the eggplants and chop. Blanch the shells in boiling water for 2 minutes, then drain upside down.

Fry the eggplant flesh, onion, garlic, pepper and mushrooms in the oil, for about 5 minutes.

Mix in the rice, cheese, egg, marjoram and seasoning. Arrange the eggplant shells in an ovenproof dish. Spoon the filling inside. Sprinkle over the nuts. Chill until ready to bake.

Heat the oven to 375 F and bake the eggplants for about 25 minutes until the filling is set and the nuts are golden brown in color.

Mousakka

(serves 8)

---

2 large eggplants, thinly sliced
6 zucchini, cut in chunks
⅔ cup olive oil, plus extra if required
1½ pounds potatoes, thinly sliced
2 onions, sliced
4 garlic cloves, crushed
⅔ cup dry white wine
2 14 ounce cans chopped tomatoes
2 tablespoons tomato paste
1 15 ounce can lentils or cook your own
2 teaspoons dried oregano
4 tablespoons chopped fresh parsley
2 cups feta cheese, crumbled
Salt and ground black pepper to taste

Sauce:
3 tablespoons butter
4 tablespoons whole wheat flour
2½ cups soy milk
2 egg substitutes, or 3 egg whites slightly beaten
4 tablespoons parmesan cheese
1 teaspoon nutmeg

Lightly salt the eggplants and zucchini in a colander and leave them to drain for 30 minutes. Rinse and pat dry.

Heat the oil until quite hot in a frying pan and quickly brown the eggplant and zucchini slices. Remove them with a slotted spoon and drain on a paper towel. This step is important to cut down on the oiliness of the eggplant. Next, brown the potato slices, remove and pat dry. Add the onion and garlic to the pan with a little extra oil, if required, and fry until lightly browned, about 5 minutes.

Pour in the wine and cook until reduced down then add the tomatoes, paste and lentils plus the liquid from the can. Stir in the herbs and season well. Cover and simmer for 15 minutes.

In a large ovenproof dish, layer the vegetables, drizzling the tomato and lentil sauce in between and scattering over the feta cheese. Finish off with a layer of eggplant slices.

Cover the vegetables with a sheet of foil and bake at 375 F for 23 minutes or until the vegetables are quite soft but not overcooked.

Meanwhile, for the sauce, put the butter, flour and milk into a saucepan all together and bring slowly to a boil, stirring or whisking constantly. It should thicken and become smooth. Season and add the nutmeg.

Remove the sauce and cool for 5 minutes then beat in the eggs. Pour it over the eggplant and sprinkle with the parmesan. If cooking ahead, cool and chill at this stage.

To finish, return to the oven uncovered and bake for another 25-30 minutes until golden brown.

Vegetable Pie
(serves 6)
◆

1 whole wheat pie shell, frozen ready-made

Filling:
1 small eggplant, peeled and chopped
2 cups chopped mushrooms
Salt to taste
2 tablespoon Spike seasoning
2 cups sliced carrots
3 tablespoons olive oil
1 onion, sliced
1 red or yellow pepper, sliced
2 garlic cloves, crushed
2 zucchini, thinly sliced
2 tomatoes, skinned and sliced
Ground black pepper to taste
2 tablespoons basil, chopped
5 ounces mozzarella cheese, sliced
2 tablespoons pine nuts

Heat the oil in a frying pan and fry the carrots, onion and pepper for 5 minutes or until tender. Add the zucchini, eggplant and mushrooms. Fry for another 10 minutes, stirring the mixture occasionally.

Stir in the tomatoes and seasoning, cook for another 3 minutes, add the basil and the garlic, then remove the pan from the heat and allow to cool.

Heat the oven to 400 F. Bake pie shell.

When ready to serve, spoon the vegetables into the case using a slotted spoon so any juices drain off and don't soak into the pastry. Top with the cheese sliced and pine nuts. Toast under a preheated broiler until golden and bubbling. Serve warm.

Zucchini Stuffed with Soy Cream Cheese

(serves 5-8)

5 medium zucchini
Water
3 tablespoons minced onion
1 cup chopped mushrooms
2 tablespoons oil
Salt and pepper to taste
2 tablespoon Spike seasoning
Dash of Cayenne
¼ teaspoon cumin
6-8 ounces soy cream cheese
Parsley, chili powder and cherry tomatoes (garnish)

Preheat oven to 325 F. Select fresh, firm, medium sized zucchini (6-8 inches). Put in a pan with enough boiling water to cover. Cook about 10 minutes or until barely tender. Lift carefully from pan and cool in cold water. Drain, slice in half lengthwise and scoop out seeded flesh into a bowl. Sauté minced onions with chopped mushrooms in oil. Drain mushrooms, saving the juice for a soup, and mix with seasonings, zucchini flesh, and soy cream cheese. Stuff zucchini halves with seasoned soy cream cheese and mushroom mixture and put in an oven-proof serving dish that has been slightly oiled. Garnish with parsley and a little chili powder. You may also garnish with a cherry tomato before or after cooking.

Vegetarian Spaghetti
(serves 4)

Sauce:
4 ounces firm tofu
2 cups spaghetti sauce mixed with 3 tablespoons of Italian seasoning
¼ pound mushrooms, thinly sliced
½ cup thinly sliced celery
3 clove garlic, pressed
½ teaspoon basil
¼ cup parmesan cheese
2 tablespoons chopped parsley
1 tablespoon chopped chives

Spaghetti:
6 ounces dry, whole wheat spaghetti noodles
2 tablespoons soy cream
½ teaspoon basil
1 tablespoon grated parmesan cheese
Parsley sprigs (garnish)

Place tofu in a medium size saucepan. Using fork, mash tofu into small chunks resembling cottage cheese. Add spaghetti sauce, mushrooms, celery, garlic and basil. Heat and stir until sauce is hot and mushrooms are cooked (about 5-10 minutes). Remove from heat and stir in parmesan cheese, parsley and chives. Keep warm.

Cook spaghetti according to package directions. Drain thoroughly and return to saucepan. Blend in soy cream and season with basil and parmesan cheese.

Pour tomato sauce all over spaghetti and mix gently to coat. Garnish with parsley sprigs.

Flavorful Vegetarian Stew
(serves 6-8)

2 cups millet
6 cups water
⅓ cup oil
¼ cup tamari sauce
1 teaspoon kelp
½ teaspoon cayenne pepper
2 cups chopped vegetables (such as potatoes, green peppers, onions, celery, carrots etc.)
Salt to taste

Dry roast millet in a large skillet or pot.* Add water, oil, and seasoning. Bring to a boil, then reduce heat. Cook over low heat, covered, for 10 minutes. Add vegetables and salt. Continue to cook until vegetables reach desired tenderness and millet is soft (like rice). Stir lightly with fork before serving.

*Dry roast means cooking over medium heat with no water or oil until browned.

Squash with Peanuts
(serves 6-8)

4 cups thinly sliced summer squash
6 tablespoons whole wheat flour
6 tablespoons butter or oil
2 cups soy cream
Salt and pepper to taste
⅓ cup grated cheddar cheese
1½ cups chopped peanuts

Cover squash with lightly slated boiling water and cook for 5 minutes. Drain. Combine flour and butter in top part of double boiler over hot water and blend. Add soy cream and cook, stirring constantly, until smooth and thickened. Add salt and pepper to taste. Stir in grated cheese and stir until cheese has melted.

Crush peanuts with rolling pan on sheet of wax paper. Do not roll them to a paste; however the texture should be uneven.

Preheat the oven to 350 F.

Arrange a layer of squash in a buttered baking dish. Spread with sauce and then sprinkle with peanuts. Repeat until all are used, ending with peanuts on top. Bake until sauce is bubbly and peanuts are lightly browned. Serve immediately.

Peanut and Potato Loaf
(serves 4)

2 cups mashed potatoes
Milk to taste
1½ cups chopped peanuts
1 cup whole wheat bread crumbs
2 egg substitute or 3 egg whites
2 chopped green onions
1 teaspoon chopped parsley
Salt to taste

Preheat oven to 350 F. Beat mashed potatoes with a little milk until they are light. Mix peanuts with potatoes. Add bread crumbs; if too stiff, add a little more milk. Whip eggs slightly and fold in with onions and parsley. Season and place in a greased baking pan. Bake for 30 minutes.

Hot Nut Loaf

(serves 4-6)

1 cup ground walnuts
1 cup ground almonds
1 cup grits soaked in 1 cup vegetable broth
3 egg substitute or 4 egg whites
½ cup wheat germ
1 cup parsley, chopped
1 teaspoon salt
1 teaspoon pepper
1 cup cooked couscous
1 medium onion sautéed in butter

Preheat oven to 350 F. Mix all ingredients together. Mixture should be slightly moist. If necessary, add more liquid or dry ingredients, whatever the case may be. Bake in oiled loaf pan for 30 minutes. Serve hot with tomato sauce or your own sauce.

Bulgur with Cabbage and Three Onions
(4-6 servings)

1 cup uncooked bulgur
1 tablespoon vegetable oil
2 medium leeks (white and light green parts) rinsed well and chopped
1 large red onion, quartered, thinly sliced
8 ounce package shredded coleslaw
3 scallions (white and light green parts), thinly sliced
1 tablespoon poppy seeds
Salt to taste
2 tablespoon Spike seasoning
½ teaspoon freshly ground pepper

In large saucepan, bring 2 cups water to a boil over high heat. Stir in bulgur, cover, reduce heat to low and simmer gently until water is absorbed (about 15 minutes).

Meanwhile, in large skillet, heat oil over medium high heat. Add leeks and onions and cook, stirring often, until softened (about 6 minutes).

Stir coleslaw cabbage and scallions into leek mixture and reduce heat to medium. Cover and cook until cabbage has wilted (about 5 minutes).

Fluff cooked bulgur with a fork, then add to onion-cabbage mixture along with poppy seeds, salt, pepper and Spike. Mix well and serve.

Veggie Burrito
(serves 4)

♦

1½ cups chopped broccoli florets
1 tablespoon olive oil
8 ounces seitan, thinly sliced
¾ cup corn kernels
½ cup diced mushrooms
1 large bell green pepper, seeded and diced
4 tomatillos, diced (optional)
1 cup salsa
2 tablespoons taco seasoning or chili powder
3 tablespoon Mexican Seasoning
Salt and freshly ground black pepper to taste
½ cup chopped fresh coriander leaves
2 cups shredded cheddar cheese
1 jalapeño pepper, minced (optional)
4 or 6 whole wheat flour tortillas
1 avocado, peeled and diced

Preheat broiler.

Heat large skillet over medium heat and add oil. When hot, place seitan slices in oil and sauté 2 to 3 minutes. Add broccoli, corn, mushrooms, green pepper, tomatillos (if using), salsa, Mexican seasonings, taco seasoning, cumin, and salt and pepper to taste. Reduce heat to medium low and cook for 10 minutes, stirring occasionally. Stir in coriander leaves, and remove from heat.

Meanwhile, sprinkle ½ cup cheese and ¼ amount of jalapeños (if using) on tortilla and broil until cheese melts and bubbles. Remove from broiler, spoon on seitan mixture, sprinkle with ¼ avocado and wrap. Repeat until remaining ingredients are all used up.

Flemish Style Red Cabbage
(serves 4)

¼ cup butter
1 large onion, coarsely chopped
1 tablespoon brown sugar
1 tablespoon salt
½ cup red wine vinegar
¼ teaspoon ground cinnamon
¼ teaspoon ground nutmeg
⅛ teaspoon ground cloves
⅛ teaspoon ground ginger
1 teaspoon black pepper
1 red cabbage, coarsely chopped
1 Granny Smith apple, peeled, cored and chopped

Melt the butter in a large, heavy pot. Add the onions and cook until they are translucent.

Add the sugar and salt, mixing well. Add the vinegar and continue to cook for 5 minutes. Add the spices and then the red cabbage, again mixing well. Cover the pot and simmer over low heat until cabbage is still a bit crunchy. Add the apple and cook until the apples are almost soft.

African Stew

(serves 6)

1 onion, chopped
1 tablespoon olive oil
4 cups vegetable broth
2 cups peeled, diced sweet potatoes or yams
1 cup cooked or canned chickpeas
1 cup brown rice, cooked
¼ teaspoon salt
¼ cup peanut butter
2 cups chopped collard greens or kale (stems removed)
2 tablespoons fresh or frozen lemon juice
½ teaspoon pepper
Dash hot chili sauce or chipotle sauce (optional)

In a large saucepan over medium heat, sauté onion in oil for 5 minutes or until beginning to brown. Add broth, sweet potatoes, chickpeas, cooked rice,* and salt and bring to a boil, then lower heat and simmer till tender. In a small bowl blend peanut butter and ½ cup of hot liquid from stew to make smooth paste. Stir peanut butter mixture into stew along with kale and cook for 5 minutes. Stir in lemon juice and pepper. Add hot sauce to taste (if using). Serve over rice or with fresh bread or rolls.

*Cook rice according to direction on package. Add 1 vegetable bullion cube to rice while cooking.

Tortilla Torte
(serves 6-8)

---

2 tablespoons virgin olive oil
12 ounces ground taco-seasoned soy meat
2 cups salsa mixed with 1 cup chopped cilantro
1½ cups pinto beans, drained and rinsed or cook your own
5 8-inch whole wheat flour tortillas
8 ounces grated cheddar cheese
1 large tomato
½ cup cilantro leaves for garnish
½ avocado, diced, for garnish
½ cup soy sour cream for garnish

Preheat oven to 425 F. Spray 10-inch round deep cake pan with nonstick cooking spray.

Heat oil in large skillet over medium heat. Sauté "meat" 3-4 minutes, add salsa and beans, and cook until heated through (about 5 minutes) stirring often.

Place 1 flour tortilla in bottom of cake pan and place about ½ cup "meat" mixture over top, spreading out to cover surface. Sprinkle with about ¼ cup cheese. Repeat the process with remainder of tortillas, filling mixture and cheese until all ingredients are used up. Spoon any remaining mixture over top, place tomato slices on mixture and sprinkle with remaining cheese.

Bake about 10 minutes, or until cheese melts, and remove from oven. Garnish with cilantro, sliced avocado, and soy sour cream. To serve, slice like a cake, including garnishes with each portion.

Chilaquileas with Beans
(serves 6)

2 cups crushed tortilla chips, preferably lime-flavored
4 plum tomatoes, coarsely chopped
4 ounce can diced green chilis
¾ cup tomatillo salsa*
2 tablespoons Mexican seasoning
1 jalapeño, minced (optional)
1 cup shredded part skim mozzarella cheese
1 cup shredded low-fat or regular cheddar cheese
3 cups canned kidney beans, drained and well rinsed or cook your own
1 bunch of scallions, thinly sliced for garnish

Preheat oven to 450 F. Spray 2 to 3 quart baking dish with nonstick cooking spray. Line bottom of dish with 1 cup crushed chips.

Heat skillet over medium high heat; cook tomatoes, green chilis, Mexican seasonings, tomatillo salsa and jalapeño (if using), 5-7 minutes. Toss cheeses together in large bowl.

Spoon half tomato mixture over chips. Layer 1 cup of cheese and all beans over top. Top with remaining chips, tomato mixture and cheese. Seal dish with foil.

Bake about 15 minutes, or until cheese melts. Garnish with cilantro and scallions. Serve hot.

Quick Tomatillo Salsa:
1 tomatillo
1 large tomato
Salt to taste
1 teaspoon Mexican seasoning
1 cup chopped cilantro
½ cup chopped onions
1 tablespoon garlic salt

Blend tomatillo and tomato in food processor until blended semi-smooth. Add other ingredients and a chopped chili if you like it hot.

Carrot Couscous with Chickpeas
(serves 4)

1 cup couscous
¾ cup carrot juice (3 medium carrots)
½ cup water
1 cup cooked chickpeas or cook your own
Salt to taste
¼ teaspoon red pepper flakes
2 teaspoon Spike seasoning

Preheat oven to 350 F.

Place couscous in an oven proof dish with a tight fitting lid. Pour juice and water over couscous; stir. Allow mixture to stand uncovered at least 15 minutes. Stir in chickpeas, salt, Spike and pepper flakes. Cover dish tightly with foil and lid. Bake for 15 minutes.

Vegetable Pockets
(serves 3-4)

¾ cup vegetable broth
1 shallot, minced
1 medium carrot, julienned
1 bunch of leeks, white part only, cleaned and sliced
1 bunch chard, about 4 cups loosely packed
2 small zucchini, sliced
Pepper to taste
2 tablespoon Spike seasoning
¼ teaspoon celery seed
¼ cup chopped parsley
1 cup grated Swiss cheese
1 sheet thawed frozen puff pastry
Salt to taste

Heat ½ cup of the broth in a large skillet. Add the shallot and cook for 5 minutes over medium heat. Add the carrot and leeks and cook 3 minutes, then add the chard, zucchini and the remaining broth and cook for 3 minutes more, remove from heat and drain well through a sieve. Add pepper, celery seed, salt, Spike, parsley and cheese. Taste and adjust seasoning.

Preheat oven to 400 F.

Gently unfold the pastry puff sheet on a lightly floured surface. Cut pastry into nine squares. Roll each square out to about 5x6 inches. Place ⅓ cup of vegetable mixture in center of square and fold corners in, pinching to seal. Place on baking sheet and bake for 15 minutes, or until pastry is crisp and lightly browned.

Tempeh Triangles with Piccata Sauce
(serves 6)

Piccata Sauce:
1½ teaspoon minced garlic
½ cup fresh lemon juice
2 cups dry red wine
1 tablespoon capers, drained
Salt and pepper to taste
1 tablespoon cornstarch dissolved in 3 tablespoons water

Tempeh Triangles:
½ cup soy milk and
1 tablespoon soy milk
1 tablespoon Dijon mustard
½ cup cornmeal
¼ cup whole wheat flour
2 tablespoons sage
2 teaspoon Spike seasoning
½ teaspoon salt
¼ teaspoon black pepper
1 8 ounce package tempeh
2 tablespoons olive oil
Lemon slices for garnish

To make Piccata Sauce: mix garlic, lemon juice, wine, capers, salt and pepper; cook about 10 minutes. Stir in cornstarch mixture; cook 3-5 minutes. Remove from heat and set aside.

To make Tempeh Triangles: whisk together soy milk and mustard in bowl. Combine Spike, cornmeal, flour, sage, salt and pepper in another bowl.

Cut each tempeh piece into 3 squares. Cut each square into two triangles. Dip triangles in soy milk mixture, then dredge in cornmeal mixture and set aside.

(continued on next page)

Heat one tablespoon oil in large skillet over medium high heat. Cook half tempeh triangles about 3 minutes per side. Add remaining oil, and repeat.

Arrange tempeh triangles on serving plates, and top with sauce. Garnish with lemon slices.

Asian Soy "Chicken" Rolls
(serves 2)

"Chicken" Rolls:
1 tablespoon plus 1 cup vegetable oil for frying
6 ounces soy "chicken" strips
1 teaspoon garlic salt
6 rice paper wrappers
1 packed cup shredded carrots
12 stems cilantro, rinsed and trimmed
½ cup fresh mint leaves
Crushed peanuts for garnish

Dipping Sauce:
⅓ cup fresh lime juice
¼ cup water
⅛ cup raw sugar, or to taste
1 teaspoon minced garlic
1 teaspoon Asian chili paste, or to taste
¼ cup shredded carrots

Chicken Rolls: Heat 1 tablespoon of oil in a large wok or skillet over medium heat. Toss "chicken" strips with garlic salt and stir fry for about 5 minutes. Remove from heat and drain on paper towels. Moisten rice paper wrappers, two sheets at a time, by dipping sheets in cold water about 10 seconds. Set aside on a flat surface until they are soft and pliable (about 1 minute). Assemble remaining ingredients in separate equal sized piles on work surface, making sure mint and cilantro stems are trimmed.

Starting with first roll, on edge closest to you, place several pieces of "chicken" on a wrapper, and layer on top shredded carrots, leafy sprigs of cilantro and several mint leaves. Wrap up roll tightly, starting at closest rounded end, taking 1 turn. Fold in each side over filling, and continue rolling up wrapper tightly into a neat packet. Repeat process until done. Heat remaining 1 cup of oil in a large wok or skillet over medium heat. Fry rolls until they are golden on all sides (about 3 minutes). Remove from heat and drain on paper towels.

Dipping sauce: Combine all ingredients, stirring until sugar dissolves. Pour onto a small serving bowl.

To serve: Arrange rolls on a serving plate, garnish them with crushed peanuts if desired and serve with dipping sauce.

Sloppy Joes
(serves 4)
◆

4 whole wheat hamburger buns
1 tablespoon virgin olive, or more as needed
1 onion, diced
12 ounces crumbled soy "ground beef"
1 teaspoon Spike seasoning
½ cup diced celery
½ cup sliced mushrooms
¾ cup barbeque sauce
¼ cup vegetable broth
Dashes hot pepper sauce to taste, optional
4 ounces shredded low-fat cheddar cheese
Salt and pepper to taste

Preheat oven to 475 F. Slice bun in half, cutting off upper third of bun to leave larger bottom section. Scoop out inner portion of each bottom section and set tops and bottoms aside on large baking sheet. Heat oil in large skillet over medium high heat. When hot, sauté onion for about 5 minutes. Stir in "ground

(continued on next page)

soy," celery, mushrooms, barbeque sauce, broth and hot pepper sauce, if using. Add Spike, salt and pepper. Cook over medium heat for 4 or 5 minutes, or until mixture is heated through. Remove from heat. Spoon equal portions of mixture onto bottom sections of buns. Sprinkle each filled bun with cheese, and spray insides of top sections of buns with nonstick cooking spray. Set tops on baking sheet, cut side up. Bake tops and bottoms for about 5 minutes, or until tops brown and cheese melts and spills down sides of buns. Remove from oven, and serve.

Curry Casserole

1 cup couscous cook according to instructions on box
1 onion, diced
1 cube soft tofu
1 clove garlic, minced
Pinch of thyme
1½ teaspoon curry powder or ½ teaspoon turmeric or
    ½ teaspoon coriander or ½ teaspoon cumin
2 potatoes, cubed
1 cup peas, steamed
1½ tablespoons olive oil
1 tablespoon caraway seeds
Salt to taste

Sauté onion, caraway seeds and potatoes in olive oil until potatoes are soft and almost thoroughly cooked. In blender, mix tofu, spices, garlic and salt. If necessary, add ½ tablespoon water to blend. Taste for seasoning. In bowl combine couscous, peas, sautéed potatoes, onion and tofu sauce until well distributed. Bake in covered casserole dish for 30-40 minutes at 350 F. Let stand for 5 minutes and serve.

For variation you can use any vegetables and spices to change this basic grain and tofu sauce casserole. Thyme, basil and parsley with bell peppers, zucchini and black olives add a nice Greek flavor.

Quinoa with Radishes
(serves 4)

1¼ cup quinoa (or substitute with millet or couscous)
3½ tablespoons cold pressed extra virgin olive oil
4 tablespoons lemon juice
2 bunches of radishes
⅔ cup ricotta cheese
2 bunches of chives
3 cloves garlic, crushed
1 large cucumber, peeled
½ cup vegetable broth
2 tablespoons fresh mint in strips
Salt and pepper to taste

Sauté the quinoa in ½ tablespoon olive oil. Add 1 tablespoon of the lemon juice to 1¾ cups water and pour over the quinoa. Add 1 teaspoon salt and bring to a boil. Boil the quinoa for 15 minutes, and then allow cooling uncovered.

Meanwhile, clean, wash and quarter the radishes. Break the cheese into chunks. Wash and chop the chives. Peel and mince the garlic. Wash the cucumber, halve it lengthwise and grate or slice very thin.

Loosely mix all of the ingredients. Mix the remaining lemon juice with the broth the remaining oil, mint, salt and pepper. Fold in and season.

Greek Potato Casserole

(serves 4)

1 bunch parsley
2 teaspoons salt 1 pinch of pepper
1 pinch oregano
1 pinch cinnamon
1 ¾ pound of potatoes for boiling
3 tablespoons cold pressed extra virgin olive oil
1 onion, chopped
½ pound zucchini, sliced
½ pound tomatoes, chopped
½ cup dry ricotta cheese
½ cup soy sour cream
½ cup soy cream

Wash and finely chop the parsley. Mix salt with pepper, oregano, cinnamon and parsley.

Wash the vegetables, peel and thinly slice the potatoes. Heat the oil in large saucepan, brown the potatoes, sprinkle the herb mixture over top, cover and cook over low heat.

Meanwhile, add the onions to the potatoes and sprinkle with some of the remaining herb mixture.

Add zucchini to the saucepan and season with the remaining herb mixture. Combine the vegetables with the tomato and cook for 15 minutes.

Blend the cheese, sour cream and cream then spread on the vegetables and cook again for 5-10 minutes.

Carrot Casserole
(serves 4)

1 pound carrots
2 cloves of garlic, smashed
2 tablespoons butter
Salt to taste
Ground pepper to taste
2 cups vegetable broth
1 cup soy milk
2 teaspoons Spike seasoning
1¼ cups coarse cornmeal or corn grits
½ cup soy sour cream
1 cup grated firm cheese (e.g., white cheddar)
Oil or butter for the baking sheet

Peel the carrots and slice in half from end to end. Melt butter in a frying pan and sauté the carrots with salt and pepper. Add 2 teaspoons vegetable broth. Simmer with the lid on for 10 minutes, then add garlic.

Remove the carrots from the saucepan. Add the remaining stock and boil with the milk.

Add the cornmeal to the liquid. Cook for 5 minutes, stirring until thick. Remove from the heat and allow mixture to cool for 15 minutes. Heat oven to 375 F. Grease a large, deep pie plate or flan pan. Fold the sour cream into the cornmeal mixture, season with Spike, salt and pepper. Spread the mixture evenly in the pie plate.

Arrange the carrots in a star shape on the polenta (corn meal mixture) and sprinkle with cheese. Bake on the middle rack for 12 minutes or until cheese has melted.

Spelt Patties with Cheese Sauce

(serves 4)

1 onion, chopped
2 cloves of garlic, smashed
⅓ pound of zucchini, grated
1 tablespoon butter
1 cup coarsely ground spelt
1⅔ cups vegetable or chicken broth
2 teaspoons Spike seasoning
1 bunch of mixed herbs
Oil for frying
1 egg substitute, beaten slightly
1 cup soy cream cheese
Salt and pepper to taste
Butter for frying

Heat the butter, then sauté the onion until translucent. Add the zucchini and spelt and sauté these briefly. Then add 1 cup stock and bring to a boil. Cover and simmer for 3 minutes. Allow mixture to cool. Add garlic.

Add the egg, ⅓ cup cream cheese and the Spike to the spelt. Mix together and season with salt and pepper.

Using damp hands shape 8 patties. Heat the oil, fry the patties briefly, place a lid on the frying pan and bake for 8-10 minutes or until cooked, turning once during cooking time. Remove patties and keep warm.

Add the remaining stock to the frying pan and dissolve the rest of the cream cheese in it. Season with salt and pepper. Serve with the patties.

Red Cabbage with Millet
(serves 4)

1 cup millet
2½ cups vegetable or chicken broth
2 small onions, chopped
2 egg substitute or 3 egg whites, beaten slightly
½ cup ricotta cheese
Salt and pepper to taste
2 pounds red cabbage, shredded
1 small sour apple, thinly sliced
1 tablespoon butter
1 small pinch powdered cloves
¼ pound blue cheese
⅓ cup soy cream
½ cup soy milk
Pinch of nutmeg
Butter for baking dish

Cook millet for 20 minutes in 1¾ broth.

Season the millet with half of the onion and then turn off heat and allow to finish cooking.

Fold eggs, ricotta, salt and pepper into the millet. Heat the butter, sauté the remaining broth, apple, salt, powdered cloves, nutmeg and pepper and cook about 20 minutes at medium heat.

Preheat the oven to 325 F. Grease the baking dish. Blend the cheese with the cream and milk, season with salt. Place the cabbage in the dish. Make dumplings from the millet mixture and place on the cabbage. Pour the cheese mixture over top and bake for 18 minutes on middle rack.

Hominy Stew

1 yellow squash, chopped
1 large can hominy
3 tablespoons olive oil
1 onion, chopped
2 garlic clove, minced
2 zucchinis, sliced
4 tomatoes, diced
4 dried New Mexico red chili pods, seed, stemmed and torn into 12 pieces
2 bay leaves, crushed
3 teaspoons Mexican seasoning
4 cups chicken or vegetable broth
2 teaspoons finely chopped fresh or dried oregano leaves
1 teaspoon finely chopped fresh or dried thyme leaves
1½ teaspoon salt
1 can of creamed corn

Place hominy in large pot of water to cover by three inches. Heat.

Heat oil in 6 quart pot over medium high heat, and sauté onion until clear (about 7 minutes). Add zucchini, yellow squash and tomatoes, and sauté 3 minutes more. Add Mexican seasonings.

Add hominy, red chili pods, bay leaves and broth. Bring to a boil, and reduce heat to low, cooking 5 minutes. Add oregano, salt, thyme, garlic and creamed corn. Serve hot in large soup bowls with warm bread.

Millan's Favorite Stuffed Zucchini

1 cup or 8 ounces of raw cheddar cheese
2 large or 4 small or 1 giant zucchini
1 small bell pepper, chopped
2 cups mushrooms, sliced
1 small onion chopped fine
2 small carrots, sliced thin
1 rib celery, chopped
Chopped insides of zucchini
4 large fresh garlic, crushed
2 teaspoons Spike seasoning
Seasoned salt
Pepper to taste
Salt to taste
Other spicy seasonings
Cooked couscous for two people

Cut zucchini lengthwise. Scoop out insides as deep as possible to make deep cavity. Sprinkle insides of zucchini with seasoned salt and pepper.

Place in container with a little water on the bottom. Cover with foil and bake for 15 minutes, at 375 F.

Meanwhile, sauté in olive oil carrots and onions together until a little soft. Then add all other ingredients except couscous, zucchini and garlic. Fry until tender. Taste to determine if enough flavoring and cooked. Then add cooked couscous and fresh garlic. Mix well.

When zucchini is completed (after the 15 minutes) scoop the veggies into zucchini cavities. Layer slices of raw cheddar cheese on top. Cover with foil. Bake 20 minutes at 350 F or until zucchini is tender. ENJOY!

BBQ Vegetables

5 pearl onions—parboil to soften
5 small red potatoes (leave skins on), par boil to soften, cut potatoes in half or quarters
2 zucchini
2 yellow squash
8 mushrooms
1 to 2 bell peppers
½ eggplant (optional)
2 tablespoons Italian seasonings
2 tablespoons Spike

Chop above to bite size. Place all of the above into bowl.

In a cup MIX WELL ½ cup olive oil, 4 cloves crushed garlic, 2 tablespoons Spike, 2 tablespoons Italian seasonings and salt to taste. Pour over all vegetables that are in the bowl. MIX WELL. Spread vegetables evenly on cookie sheet and place under broiler to brown. With a pancake turner, turn veggies over to brown other side.

Tomatoes Stuffed with Corn Soufflé

(serves 4)

♦

These are much easier to make than a traditional soufflé and are delicious served with a green salad and a slice of whole grain bread. Choose firm, ripe tomatoes that will sit flat, not tip over.

4 large, firm, ripe tomatoes, ¾ to 1 pound each
2½ cups fresh corn (about 5 ears) or 2 cans corn
3 large egg substitute or 4 egg whites
¼ cup plus 1 tablespoon grated parmesan cheese or soy parmesan cheese
¼ cup finely chopped fresh basil or 2 tablespoons dried basil
2 teaspoons Spike seasoning

Preheat oven to 400 F. Spray 9x13 inch baking pan with cooking spray; set aside.

Cut half inch off top of tomatoes. Scoop out centers of tomatoes, leaving shells intact. Lightly sprinkle insides of shells with salt. Place cut side down on paper towels; let drain for 30 minutes.

Put 1½ cups corn, eggs, and ¼ cup parmesan cheese in food processor or blender; puree until smooth. Pour into bowl, and stir in remaining corn and basil. Season to taste with salt, pepper and Spike.

Set tomato shells, cut side up, in baking dish. Fill each with corn mixture, and sprinkle with remaining parmesan cheese.

Bake 45 minutes, or until filling is set and tops are browned and slightly puffed. Remove, and let cool about 5 minutes. Carefully transfer tomatoes to plates. Serve immediately.

Indian Spiced Cauliflower
(serves 8)

1½ teaspoons olive oil
¼ teaspoon crushed red pepper
5 cloves garlic, minced
1 medium onion, chopped
2 ribs celery, sliced
1½ tablespoon grated ginger root
4 medium red potatoes, sliced into ¼ inch wedges
1 16 ounce package Hickory Baked tofu, sliced
6 ounces mushrooms, sliced
1 small head cauliflower (1¼ pounds) separated into florets
¼ teaspoon turmeric
¼ cup dry sherry
1 14½ ounce can stewed tomatoes
¼ cup chopped fresh cilantro
⅓ cup vegetarian or chicken broth

Warm oil and crushed red pepper in an electric frying pan or a 5 quart sauce pan over medium high heat for one minute. Add onions, celery, and ginger and sauté in hot oil for 3 minutes. Add the potatoes and cook mixture for 8 minutes, until potatoes soften. Add the sliced, baked tofu and the mushrooms and cauliflower. Cook mixture 5 minutes or until cauliflower is tender. Add the turmeric, sherry, tomatoes, and remaining ingredients. Stir to mix thoroughly, reduce heat to medium low and simmer for 10 minutes or until veggies are tender, stirring occasionally. Add garlic.

Lumpia

(makes 15 lumpia)

2 tablespoons vegetable oil
2 cloves of garlic, minced
1 onion, sliced
1 pound soy sausage
½ pound green beans, julienned
2 carrots, julienned
1 tablespoon soy sauce or Bragg's liquid aminos
1 cup bean sprouts
Salt to taste
15 lumpia or wonton wrappers
Vegetable oil for frying

Heat oil in a skillet and sauté onions until tender. Add soy sausage and sauté until browned. Add green beans and carrots and cook until tender yet crisp (about 5 minutes). Remove from heat. Season with soy sauce. When mixture is cool, add bean sprouts and garlic. Season with salt, to taste.

To assemble lumpia:

Carefully separate wrappers. To prevent them from drying out, cover unused wrappers with a moist paper towel. Lay one wrapper on a clean surface. Place 2-3 tablespoons of the filling near the edge closest to you. Roll edge toward the middle. Fold in both sides and continue rolling. Moisten opposite edge with water to seal. Repeat with other wrappers. Lumpia can be frozen until ready to use.

Heat oil to 350 F. Deep fry lumpia until golden brown (3-5 minutes on each side). Drain on paper towels. Serve with sweet and sour sauce or vinegar dipping sauce.

Tempura Vegetables with Dipping Sauce
(serves 4-6)

1 medium zucchini, sliced in thin sticks
1 red pepper, seeded and cut in wedges
3 large mushrooms, quartered
4 carrots peeled and sliced in sticks
1 fennel bulb, cut in wedges with root attached
Oil, for deep frying

Sauce:
3 tablespoons soy sauce or Bragg's liquid aminos
1 tablespoon medium dry sherry
1 teaspoon sesame seed oil
Few shreds fresh ginger or scallion

Batter:
1 egg substitute or 2 egg whites
1 cup whole wheat flour
¾ cup cold water
Salt and ground pepper to taste

Prepare all the vegetables and lay out on a tray, together with sheets of paper towel for draining the vegetables after cooking.

Mix the sauce ingredients together by whisking them in a bowl or shaking them together in a sealed jar. Pour into a bowl.

Half fill a deep frying pan with oil and preheat to a temperature of about 375 F. Quickly whisk the batter ingredients together but don't overbeat them. It doesn't matter if the batter is a little lumpy.

Fry the vegetables in stages by dipping a few quickly into the batter and lowering into the hot oil in a wire basket. Fry for just a minute until golden brown and crisp. Drain on the paper towel.

Repeat until all the vegetables are fried. Keep those you have cooked uncovered, in a warm oven while you fry the rest. Serve the vegetables on a large platter along side the dipping sauce.

Aromatic Vegetables

(serves 8)

2 tablespoons olive oil
2 cups chopped onion
2 tablespoons minced garlic
2 tablespoons minced ginger
2 tablespoons curry powder
3 russet potatoes, diced (1/2 inch)
4 carrots, peeled, halved lengthwise and diced (1 inch)
1 butternut squash, peeled, seeded and cubed (½ inch)
1 fennel bulb, cubed (½ inch)
1 medium sized cauliflower, broken into small florets
2 cups green beans, cut (1½ inches)
2 cups vegetable broth
2 tablespoons honey
4 whole cloves
1 cinnamon stick (3 inches long)
1 can of chickpeas, drained or cook your own
½ cup chopped cilantro leaves
2 tablespoons chopped mint leaves

Heat oil in a large heavy pot over low heat. Wilt the onions, stirring occasionally, about 5 minutes; add the ginger to mellow for the last three minutes. Add the curry powder and cook, stirring, for an additional 2 minutes. Add the vegetables, broth, honey, cloves and cinnamon stick. Bring to a boil, reduce the heat to medium low and simmer uncovered, until the vegetables are tender (about 10 minutes). Stir in the chickpeas and heat. Add garlic. Discard the cinnamon stick and cloves. Add the cilantro, sprinkle with chopped mint leaves and serve.

Sautéed Spinach with Garlic
(serves 4)

Salt to taste
1 tablespoon butter
8 cups of tightly packed spinach leaves (about 2 bunches or 2 5-7 ounce bags of spinach leaves)
2 tablespoons olive oil or other neutral flavored oil
1 tablespoon minced garlic
1 tablespoon and 1 teaspoon grated ginger root
1 teaspoon sesame oil
Ground black pepper to taste
2 teaspoon Spike seasoning
1 tablespoon sesame seeds (optional)

Bring 3 quarts of water to a boil. Add salt, butter, and spinach and cook until just barely wilted, about 20 seconds. Drain the spinach and spread it on a wire rack over a baking sheet to cool as quickly as possible. Place the spinach in a clean kitchen towel and gently squeeze out the excess water. Set aside.

Heat the oil in a large pan over medium heat. Add the spinach and ginger. Sauté for one minute, until heated through. Add the sesame oil and stir. Taste and adjust the seasoning with salt and pepper. Transfer the spinach to a warmed serving bowl and add Spike and garlic.

If desired, sprinkle sesame seeds on top.

Potato Almond Loaf
(serves 4)

1 medium onion, chopped
1 cup thinly sliced mushrooms
4 tablespoons butter
4 medium potatoes, grated
1 cup slivered almonds
1 egg substitute or 2 egg whites
½ cup soy milk

Preheat oven to 375 F. Sauté onion with mushrooms in butter until transparent. Wash and grate potatoes. Mix all ingredients thoroughly and turn into greased loaf pan 9x5 inches. Bake for 1 hour.

Stuffed Squash
(serves 6)

———◆———

1 large squash, big enough to stuff
2 tablespoons olive oil
3 onions, minced
6 celery ribs (with leaves)
1 teaspoon salt or to taste
1 cup vegetable or chicken broth
1 cup water chestnuts, from can, chopped
3 cups cooked brown rice, millet or bulgur
Cayenne pepper to taste
1 teaspoon paprika
1 teaspoon crushed sage
½ cup chopped almonds

Bake squash for 1-2 hours and cool. Split squash in half and scoop out seeds and membrane. Heat 1 tablespoon oil in skillet and sauté onion. When it is lightly browned, add celery and sauté a few minutes more. Add salt and ½ cup of broth. Simmer for 10 minutes. Combine with remaining ingredients. Fill squash cavities and brush sides with remaining oil. Place in a roasting pan and cover with foil. Bake for 30 minutes or until all is tender.

Black-Eyed Peas and Rice

1 cup dried black-eyed peas, sorted, rinsed and soaked overnight*
1 bay leaf
3 cups cooked brown rice
Salt to taste
Freshly ground black pepper to taste

Sauce:
1 tablespoon olive oil
1 heaping tablespoon whole wheat flour
1 large onion, sliced
1 cup tomato paste
½ teaspoon freshly ground nutmeg

Discard pea soaking water; rinse peas. Refill pot with fresh, cold water (cover peas to a depth of 2-3 inches). Add a bay leaf if desired; bring to a boil, reduce heat and simmer peas gently with pot cover ajar until tender (about 1 hour). Add more water if necessary. Water should be nearly evaporated at end of cooking time. Discard bay leaf . Add cooked rice, salt and pepper to taste at end of cooking time.

Sauce:
Heat oil in skillet. Add flour and mix to make roux. Cook over low heat, stirring constantly until roux browns slightly (about 2 minutes). Add onion; cook until browned. Add tomato paste and nutmeg; stir until well mixed. Add water to desired consistency (sauce should be thick and not soupy). Serve over black-eyed peas and rice.

*To quick soak dried beans, cover to a depth of 2 inches with fresh cold water in a large pot. Bring to a boil; cook 2-3 minutes. Turn heat off; let beans soak for 1 hour. Pour off soaking water and proceed with recipe.

Scalloped Potatoes

4 tablespoons butter
8 medium potatoes, sliced thin
1½ large onion, chopped
1 cup soy cream
1 cup soy milk
Salt and pepper to taste

Layer ¼ of the sliced potatoes on bottom of baking dish. Sprinkle ¼ of the onions, salt, pepper and dab small chunks of butter (1 tablespoon) on top.

Repeat the above process until all of the potatoes are used.

Heat soy cream and soy milk combined till scalded. Pour over potato layers. Bake 375 F for 30 minutes or until potatoes are tender.

Confetti Rice
(serves 6)

———◆———

1 cup cooked brown rice
1 teaspoon Mexican seasoning
2 15 ounce cans rinsed and drained kidney beans or
   cook your own
1½ cups corn
1 cup diced red onion
1 cup diced red or green bell pepper
1 cup finely chopped fresh cilantro
2 tablespoons seeded and diced jalapeño pepper if desired
1 tablespoon olive oil
3 tablespoons fresh lime juice

Cook brown rice according to package directions with Mexican seasoning. Fluff with fork. Add beans, corn, onion, bell peppers, cilantro and jalapeño to the rice. Stir in oil and enough lime juice to give a zesty edge. Serve warm or at room temperature.

Delicious Stuffed Rolled Eggplant

1 eggplant, sliced ¼ inch thick lengthwise
Extra virgin olive oil
Garlic salt and pepper to taste
2 teaspoons dried parsley or Italian seasoning
6 ounces soft cheese (goat is recommended)
2 tomatoes, chopped
Italian dressing

Brush each side of eggplant with oil, pepper and garlic salt. Broil directly under broiler until roasted. Turn over with a pancake turner and repeat.

Cool slightly.

Crumble the cheese and mix with the herbs. Spread a little of the cheese evenly onto each eggplant until it's all used up. Roll like a burrito and place in a row onto plate. Place the tomatoes encircling the rolled eggplants. Pour a little Italian dressing on each rolled eggplant and tomatoes and serve.

Spicy Black-Eyed Peas
(serves 8)

- 1 pound dry black-eyed peas
- 6 cups water
- 2 garlic cloves, pressed or minced
- 2 medium onions, chopped
- 1 bell pepper, diced
- 1 teaspoon salt
- ½ teaspoon freshly ground black pepper
- ½ teaspoon raw sugar
- ½ teaspoon dried oregano, crushed
- ½ teaspoon dried thyme, crushed
- 26 ounces canned chopped tomatoes, undrained
- 1 can (4 ounces) diced green chilis, undrained
- ¼ cup red wine vinegar

Combine black-eyed peas and water in a large pot and bring to a rapid boil. Allow to boil for 2 minutes, then remove from the heat. Cover and allow to stand for 1 hour.

While the black-eyed peas are soaking, combine the garlic, onions and bell pepper in a skillet and cook over low heat, covered until the onion is translucent, adding a little water as necessary to prevent scorching.

Add the cooked onion mixture and all remaining ingredients to the black eyed peas and bring to a boil. Reduce heat to low and cook, covered, for 1½-2 hours, or until peas are soft.

Butternut Stew with Tofu and Pine Nuts

4 cups corn
4 cups peeled and diced butternut squash
4 cloves garlic, minced
1 teaspoon salt
½ teaspoon pepper
4 cups water, dissolved with 2 vegetable or chicken bouillon cubes
4 tablespoons olive oil
1 firm tofu, diced
½ cup whole wheat flour
½ cup pine nuts
2 scallions, minced, for garnish

Place corn in blender or food processor, and puree until coarse. Transfer corn to heavy sauce pan and add squash, garlic, salt, pepper and water. Bring to a boil over medium heat, stir to mix and cook until squash is tender.

Meanwhile, heat large skillet over medium heat and add oil. Toss diced tofu in flour, and sauté until browned on all sides. Add pine nuts. When squash is tender, add tofu and pine nuts, stir and continue cooking 5 minutes. Remove from heat, garnish with scallions.

Coconut Macaroons

(Makes 36 cookies)

2 large white eggs
¼ teaspoon cream of tartar
Dash of salt
½ cup raw sugar
½ teaspoon vanilla extract
3 cups (about 12 ounces) shredded coconut

Preheat the oven to 325 F. In a large bowl, combine the egg whites, cream of tartar and salt. Beat until soft peaks form, and then gradually add the sugar, continuing to beat until the mixture is stiff and glossy. Add the vanilla extract at the end.

Fold the coconut into the meringue, then scoop onto greased parchment-lined cookie sheets in 1½ inch mounds.

Bake for 18 to 22 minutes, until the coconut is toasted golden brown and the centers of the cookie sheet are set. The macaroons should still be moist inside.

Remove from the oven and allow cookies to cool on the pan for 5-10 minutes before transferring to a rack to finish cooling completely. Store in an air-tight container.

Louise Edward's Peach Cobbler

(Serves 6)

◆

4 cups peeled and sliced peaches (about 6 medium peaches) or from can, unsweetened
1 tablespoon lemon juice
½ cup raw sugar
4 tablespoons butter
1 cup all purpose flour
½ teaspoons baking powder
1 teaspoon baking soda
½ teaspoon salt
1 cup soy milk
Pinch of nutmeg

Preheat oven to 375 F.

Toss the peaches with lemon juice and ¼ cup sugar and nutmeg in a mixing bowl. Let the mixture stand for 10 minutes.

Meanwhile, heat the butter in a small saucepan, and pour the melted butter into a 2 quart baking dish. Swirl the butter around to coat the bottom of the dish and set aside.

Combine the flour, the remaining ¼ cup sugar, baking powder, baking soda, pinch of nutmeg and salt in a mixing bowl.
Stir in the milk and mix well to combine.

Pour the batter into the prepared dish. Spoon out the peach mixture over the batter, and do not stir.

Bake for 45-50 minutes, or until the batter is set and lightly browned. Remove from the oven, and let cool slightly. Serve warm if desired.

Hemp Seed Balls

20 pitted, soft dates
1 cup raw cashews (powdered in food processor)
2-3 tablespoons vanilla
3 tablespoons raw coconut butter
½ cup hemp seeds
Pinch of salt

Throw the dates, vanilla and salt into a food processor and mix thoroughly into a paste. Blend in the cashew powder (about one cup—just enough to dry out the mixture a little bit). Add the coconut butter (liquefy it in warm water before adding if it is solid). Roll into small, 1 inch round balls, and cover with hemp seeds. Place into the freezer until ready to serve. Absolutely decadent.

Orange Honey Cake

3 egg substitutes
¾ cup raw sugar
½ cup honey
3 tablespoons vegetable oil
2 teaspoons instant coffee granules
⅓ cup (3 ounces) frozen orange juice concentrate (thawed)
1¾ cups all purpose flour
1 teaspoon baking powder
1 teaspoon ground cinnamon
½ teaspoon ground all allspice
⅛ teaspoon salt
1 teaspoon baking soda

Preheat oven to 300 F.

Mix eggs, sugar, honey and vegetable oil with an electric mixer until blended. Dissolve coffee in ½ cup warm water then mix it into the batter along with the orange juice. In a separate bowl, mix together flour, baking soda, baking powder, cinnamon, allspice and salt. Add to batter. Mix for 1 minute or until smooth. Pour into greased 9x5x3 inch loaf pan.

Bake for 65-75 minutes or until toothpick inserted in center comes out clean. Remove from rack; cool 10 minutes. Invert and cool completely.

Cream Banana Date Milkshake

1 10 ounce tofu
1 ripe banana
1 cup apple juice
4 pitted dates

Blend until smooth.

Noodle Kugel

Some believe that kugel originated in Persia, today's Iran, and then spread to Eastern Europe.

8 ounces thin soup noodles
1 cup raw sugar
2 sticks of butter softened at room temperature
1 pound low fat cottage cheese
2 cups soy sour cream at room temperature
8 ounces soy cream cheese softened at room temperature
1 cup soy milk
6 slightly beaten egg whites
Ground cinnamon to taste

Preheat oven to 450 F. Grease 9x13 inch baking dish and set aside.

Cook noodles for 5 minutes in lightly salted, boiling water. Drain well and set aside to cool. Combine sugar, butter, cottage cheese, sour cream, cream cheese and milk in large bowl and mix well. Stir in noodles and eggs, and sprinkle top with cinnamon. Place in baking dish.

Bake for 5 minutes, reduce heat to 350 F and continue baking for 45-50 minutes more, or until lightly browned on top.

Golden Harvest Cake

1 cup (2 sticks) butter, softened
1½ cups dark brown sugar
4 egg substitutes
2 cups cooked butternut squash, pureed or smashed well
2 cups finely diced raw green apple
2 cups all purpose flour
2½ teaspoons baking soda
1½ teaspoons baking powder
1 tablespoon ground cinnamon
1 teaspoon salt
1 cup raisins
1 cup chopped pecans

Pecan Praline Frosting:
1 cup dark brown sugar
½ cup soy cream
½ cup butter
1 tablespoon vanilla extract
3 cups confectioners' sugar
2 cups coarsely chopped pecans
1 cup pecan halves for garnish, if desired

Preheat oven to 350 F. Butter and flour three 9 inch round cake pans.

To make cake: cream butter and sugar until light and fluffy. Add egg substitutes, and beat for 2 minutes. Add pureed squash and apple, and mix thoroughly.

Mix flour, baking soda, baking powder, cinnamon and salt in separate bowl. Mix together and add butter mixture in 4 separate batches. Fold in raisins and chopped pecans.

Bake cake 55 minutes, or until toothpick inserted in center come out clean. Remove from oven and cool.

To make frosting: place brown sugar and soy cream in saucepan and bring to a boil over medium heat. Reduce heat to low, and cook for 10 minutes. Remove from heat and add butter and vanilla. Set aside to cool, but do not stir. Place frosting in a bowl and beat in confectioners' sugar, a little at a time, until spreading consistency. Fold in chopped nuts, saving pecan halves for top of cake.

Place bottom cake layer on a plate, and spread frosting over it, letting frosting drizzle down sides of cake. Repeat with remaining two layers. Alternate method: frost each cake layer, both sides and top. If frosting begins to harden, dip spatula into warm water to make frosting easier to spread.

Lareesa's Favorite Custard

3 eggs, slightly beaten
⅓ cup raw sugar
Dash of salt
1 teaspoon vanilla
1½ cups soy milk, scalded
Ground nutmeg

Preheat oven to 350 F. Mix eggs, sugar, salt, and vanilla. Stir in milk gradually. Pour into six 6 ounce custard cups or casserole dish; sprinkle with nutmeg. Place in pan of hot water to within ½ inch of tops of custard cups or casserole.

Bake until knife inserted halfway between center and edge comes out clean, about 45 minutes. Remove cups from water. Serve warm or chilled.

Raw Apple Cake
(Serves 8)

1 cup soy milk
4 egg whites
2 cups raw sugar
1½ cups oil
3 cups all purpose flour
1 teaspoon baking soda
1 teaspoon salt
1 teaspoon cinnamon
1 teaspoon vanilla extract
3 cups shredded apples
1 cup pecans
Powdered sugar

In a large bowl beat eggs. Beat in sugar and milk. Add oil, flour, soda, salt and cinnamon. Add vanilla and mix well. Stir in chopped apples and nuts by hand. Pour onto greased and floured 9 inch tube pan. Bake at 350 F for 60 minutes. Remove cake from pan and place on rack to cool. When cool, place on serving plate and dust well with powdered sugar.

Apple-Lemon Fritters
(Serves 4-6)

½ cup soymilk
3 egg whites
2 tablespoons melted butter
¼ cup cornmeal
1½ cups all purpose flour
1 teaspoon baking powder
1 teaspoon salt
2 cups (about 1½ apples) diced apples
1 teaspoon ground cinnamon
1 tablespoon lemon zest
1 tablespoon raw sugar
2 cups vegetable oil for frying, or more as needed

Place milk, eggs, and butter in a large mixing bowl and beat until well combined. Fold in cornmeal, flour, salt and baking powder and stir until well combined. Fold in apples, cinnamon, lemon zest and sugar.

Heat oil in large skillet or deep saucepan over medium heat. When the oil is hot spoon batter into oil, about ¼ cup at a time, and fry until golden brown on both sides for 3-4 minutes. Remove from oil and place on several layers of paper towels to blot out excess oil. Repeat until batter is all used up.

Place fritters on individual plates and serve with a variety of toppings.

My Dear Louise's Sweet Potato Pie

(Serves 8)

───◆───

½ cup soy cream
2 cups freshly cooked and mashed sweet potatoes,
   peels removed
1 tablespoon butter, melted
⅓ cup honey, or to taste
½ teaspoon ground cinnamon
½ teaspoon ground nutmeg
¼ teaspoon salt
¾ cup egg substitute, beaten
1 9 inch whole wheat pie crust, chilled
   (purchase from freezer section at grocers)
Ground cinnamon for garnish (optional)

Preheat oven to 400 F.

In a large bowl, mix together the ingredients except the pie crust and cinnamon. Process the sweet potato mixture in a blender or food processor until smooth. Combine all and mix well.

Pour the filling into a chilled pie crust and bake 10 minutes. Reduce oven temperature to 300 F and bake 45-50 minutes more. Let cool. Serve the pie chilled or at room temperature, with a sprinkle of cinnamon.

Pineapple Upside Down Cake

Melt ⅓ cup butter. Mix ¼ cup honey completely into melted butter and spread it over a 10 inch skillet. Arrange 1 can of drained, naturally sweetened pineapple slices over butter mixture and save the juice. Dot the center of each pineapple slice with a half of a maraschino cherry. Set aside.

3 egg whites
½ cup honey
6 tablespoons juice from canned pineapple
1 teaspoon vanilla
1 cup whole all purpose flour
1 teaspoon baking powder
¼ teaspoon salt

Preheat oven to 350 F.

Beat egg whites and add honey, juice, and vanilla and mix completely.

In a separate bowl mix together, flour, baking powder and salt. Combine the liquid mixture with the flour mixture and mix completely. Carefully pour the batter over the pineapple slices making sure they are completely covered. Bake until a tooth pick inserted into the center of the cake comes out clean, approximately 45 minutes. Immediately invert cake onto a serving plate, displaying the pineapple slices.

Bump and Crunch Cookies

¾ cup rolled oats
¼ teaspoon baking powder
¼ cup raisins
¼ cup carob chips
½ teaspoon vanilla
¼ cup sesame or safflower oil
¾ cup whole wheat pastry flour
¾ cup barley malt or rice syrup or natural maple syrup
½ cup chopped nuts
3 tablespoons water

Preheat oven to 375 F.

In large mixing bowl, toss together rolled oats, flour, baking powder, raisins, carob chips and chopped nuts. Stir in the oil, malt or syrup, vanilla and water until well mixed.

Using a soup spoon to scoop out cookie batter, drop on lightly oiled cookie sheet. Wait about 5 minutes then shape the batter into cookies by hand, wetting hands with water if batter is sticky. Bake for 15-30 minutes, depending on size of the cookies.

Banana Bread
(8 servings)

◆

2 cups mashed bananas
3 egg whites
1 cup vegetable oil
1 teaspoon vanilla
2 cups whole wheat flour
1 cup raw sugar
1 teaspoon baking soda
1 teaspoon salt
1 cup chopped walnuts

Preheat oven to 350 F.

In a bowl, combine the bananas, egg whites, oil and vanilla, and mix well. In another bowl, sift together the flour, sugar, baking soda and salt, and add to the banana mixture. Stir in nuts.

Pour the batter into a greased and floured loaf pan. Bake for 50 minute or until done.

Gingerbread
(Serves 6)

⅓ cup butter, softened to room temperature
1 cup molasses
1 egg substitute
½ cup buttermilk
2 cups whole wheat flour
½ teaspoon salt
1½ teaspoons baking soda
1½ teaspoons ground ginger
¼ teaspoon ground cloves

Preheat oven to 350 F.

In a medium size mixing bowl, blend together butter and molasses. Add egg substitute and buttermilk. Mix dry ingredients together. Stir in completely with other ingredients. Pour mixture into a well buttered 8x8x2 inch baking pan and bake for 30-35 minutes or until toothpick inserted in center comes out clean. Cool in pan.

Applesauce Soufflé
(Serves 4)

1¼ cups unsweetened applesauce
2 tablespoons natural maple syrup
½ teaspoon cinnamon
2 teaspoons raisins
3 egg whites

Preheat oven to 350 F.

Blend applesauce with syrup and cinnamon. Spoon 1 tablespoon of applesauce into the bottom of four 6 ounce custard cups. Top with raisins. Beat egg whites until stiff but not dry. Fold half into remaining applesauce and blend well. Fold remaining whites into applesauce very gently. Spoon into custard cups and sprinkle tops with cinnamon.

Bake about 15-20 minutes, until puffed and browned. Serve immediately.

Healthy Tasty Carrot Cake

1 cup all purpose flour
1 cup whole wheat flour
2 teaspoons baking soda
½ teaspoon salt
2 teaspoons cinnamon
4 egg whites
¼ cup vegetable or healthy grapeseed oil
¾ cup soy cream
¾ cup raw sugar
¼ cup raw honey
2 teaspons vanilla extract
3 cups grated carrots
1 apple, cored, shredded
1 cup shredded coconut
½ cup raisins
1 cup chopped walnuts or pecans

Preheat oven to 350 F. Oil and flour tube cake pan.

In large bowl, mix well all dry ingredients. In another bowl beat slightly egg whites and combine with all wet ingredients, except carrots, apple, coconut, raisins and walnuts. Beat well together. Add carrots, apple, coconut, raisins and walnuts.

(continued on next page)

Combine dry ingredients to carrot mixture and mix well only till all is moistened.

Fill cake pan evenly with above. Bake for 45 minutes or until toothpick inserted comes out clean. Remove from pan inserting knife to separate cake from pan and place onto plate. Sprinkle lightly on top with powdered sugar.

Peanut Butter Cookies
(2 dozen cookies)

1 cup nutty peanut butter
1 cup oil
1 cup raw sugar
2 eggs
2 cups whole wheat flour
1 teaspoon vanilla
2 teaspoons baking soda

Preheat oven to 350 F.

In a large bowl, combine flour, salt, baking soda and sugar. Cream oil, vanilla, peanut butter and eggs. Gradually add in flour mixture. Form into little balls by teaspoonfuls. Place on cookie sheet. Press each ball with fork. Bake at 375 F for approximately 10 minutes.

Pumpkin Rice Pudding
(Serves 6)

2 cups pumpkin or winter squash, cooked
1 cup soy milk
3-5 tablespoons honey
1 tablespoon tahini
1½ teaspoons pumpkin pie spice
1-2 egg substitutes
2 cups brown rice, cooked
½ cups raisins

Blend pumpkin, soy milk, honey, tahini, pumpkin pie spice, and egg substitute until smooth. Combine with rice and raisins. Pour into a greased casserole dish and place in pan of hot water. Bake 350 F for 1 hour or until an inserted knife comes out clean. Serve warm or chilled, with yogurt if desired.

Fruit and Nut Balls
(3 dozen)

¾ cup ground pitted prunes
½ cup finely chopped pecans or cashews
¼ cup honey
½ cup raisins
¼ cup sunflower seeds
Shredded coconut

Mix together all ingredients except the coconut. Shape into small balls using a scant teaspoonful for each. Roll in coconut and chill.

Easy Bread Pudding

4 slices whole wheat bread, cubed
¼ cup raisins*
1 cup nut milk or soy cream
½ cup Sweet Basic or raw sugar
⅛ teaspoon cinnamon

Cut bread into cubes. In an oven-proof bowl, mix together the cinnamon, milk, Sweet Basic, or raw sugar and raisins. Fold in bread cubes. Pack down slightly. Bake, covered, at 375 F for 45 minutes.

*Chopped dates, apples, nuts, etc. may be substituted.

Nutty Cookies

1½ cups brown rice flour or all purpose flour
1 cup almonds chopped
¼ cup sesame seeds
¼ teaspoon baking powder
¼ cup sesame or safflower oil
⅓ cup rice syrup or natural maple syrup
½ teaspoon almond extract
3 tablespoons water

In large mixing bowl, toss together the rice flour, almonds, sesame seeds, and baking powder. Stir in oil, syrup, almond extract and water until well mixed.

Roll cookie batter into balls by hand, wetting hands if batter is sticky. Place balls on lightly oiled cookie sheet. Flatten each ball with palm of hand or a fork. You can decorate each cookie with a whole almond. Bake for 15-20 minutes depending on the size of the cookies. These cookies will remain rather pale except for the edges.

Zucchini Crown Bread
(Serves 8)

◆

1 pound zucchini, coarsely grated
1 tablespoon plus 1 teaspoon salt
5 cups all purpose flour
2 packages fast action yeast
4 tablespoons parmesan cheese
2 tablespoons olive oil
Lukewarm water, to mix
Soy milk, to glaze
Sesame seeds, to garnish

Spread out the zucchini in a colander and sprinkle lightly with 1 teaspoon salt. Allow it to drain for 30 minutes, then pat dry.

Mix the flour, 1 tablespoon salt, yeast and parmesan together.

Stir in the oil and zucchini and add enough lukewarm water to make a good, firm dough.

Knead the dough on a lightly floured surface until it is smooth, then return it to the mixing bowl. Cover it with oiled plastic wrap and leave it to rise in a warm place.

Meanwhile, grease and line a 9 inch round cake pan and then preheat the oven to 400 F.

When the dough has doubled in size, turn it out of the bowl, punch it down and knead it lightly. Break into eight balls, rolling each one and placing them in the cake pan next to each other. Brush the tops with soy milk and sprinkle with sesame seeds.

Allow to rise again, then bake for 25 minutes or until slightly golden brown. Cool slightly in the pan, then turn out the bread to cool completely.

Nut Milk

1 cup raw nuts (cashews blend the smoothest)
4-6 cups of water
2-4 tablespoons rice syrup (optional) or natural maple syrup
¼ teaspoon vanilla (optional)

Soak nuts in 2 cups of water for a few hours or overnight in the refrigerator. Put nuts and soaking water in blender and blend on high until smooth. Add 2-4 more cups of water (depending on strength desired), rice syrup and vanilla (for sweeter milk), and blend. Refrigerate in covered container or jar. Keeps for about three days.

Hot Carob Delight

1 recipe nut milk
¼ cup carob powder
1½ teaspoons vanilla
⅓ to ½ cup raw sugar to taste
½ teaspoon cinnamon powder

Put carob powder, vanilla, sweetener and cinnamon with 2 cups of nut milk in blender and process until very smooth. Heat carob mixture with remainder of nut milk in saucepan and stir until blended. Heat over medium flame until warm. Serve.

This can also be made as a shake with 1-2 frozen bananas.

Biography

In 1981 Millan Chessman became a Certified Entero Hydrotherapist and received her bachelor's degree in nutritional science. She operated the largest detox alternative health clinic in San Diego. Millan authored the first book written about modern day professional internal cleansing, *Cleanse Internally to Become Younger.* Millan is a credentialed instructor through International Association of Colon Therapists (I-ACT). She has traveled worldwide and has given health talks and instruction about nutrition, fasting and internal cleansing on television and radio. Looking half her age, her excellent health at age sixty-six shows she is one who practices what she preaches. Millan is listed in *Who's Who in the Nationwide Register of Executives.* She is the creator of Millan's Home Internal Cleansing Kit sold worldwide and operates a Supervised Fasting Retreat in San Diego and Julian, California. Millan's nutritional consultation specializes in permanent weight loss. Her expertise may be seen on her Web site www.coloniccleanse.com.

SHE IS AVAILABLE AS A GUEST SPEAKER WITH HER SALSA STEP AEROBICS PERFORMANCE AT NO CHARGE. Call 1-800-311-8222.

Index

Sauces and Dressings
Cream Sauce, 7
Cucumber Dressing, 3
Dipping Sauce for Tempura, 148
Eggplant Cream, 5
Emergency Dressing, 4
Green Salad Dressing, 11
Guacamole Chip Dip, 9
Hummus, 8
Hummus Trio, 10
Italian Salad Dressing, 11
Peanut Dressing, 50
Pepper Yogurt Sauce, 86
Piccata Sauce, 133-134
Salad Dressing, Millan's Healthy & Delicious, 5
Spicy Sesame Sauce, 6
Sweet and Sour Sauce, 3
Tomatillo Salsa, Quick, 131
Yogurt Dressing (Arabic), 4

Side Dishes
Celery and Peanut Butter, 21
Collard Greens, Magic Johnson's Southern-Style, 16
Creamy Corn Salsa, 15
French Fried Potatoes, Un-fried, 21
Fried Green Tomatoes, Basic, 20
Hot Carrots, 18
Toast, Breakfast, 21
Spinach Pesto, 19
Sugar Snap Pea Sauté with Mushrooms and Corn, 17
Sweet Potato Chips, 18

Soups
Barley Soup, 37
Baked Pumpkin Soup, 29
Chickpea, Lentils and Bulgur Wheat Soup, 36
Corn and Sweet Potato Soup, 28
Corn Chowder, 26
Lentil Soup, 31
Minestrone Soup, Jeff's Favorite, 35
Portuguese Soup, 32
Potato Soup, Chunky, 33
Split Pea Medley, 25
Sweet Potato Coconut Soup, 27
Vegetable Chowder, Delicious, 30
White Bean Soup, Quick, 34

Salads
Baby Pea Salad, 49
Beet Apple Salad, Millan's, 57
Broccoli Salad, Roxanne's Popular, 57
Caesar's Salad, 56
Chef's Spinach Salad, 53
Coleslaw, 46
Couscous Salad, 47
Cranberry Waldorf Salad, 52
Curried Kale Salad, 41
Delicious Salad, 53
Kale Delight, 58
Kashi Vegetable Salad, 54
Marinated Cucumber Salad, 59
Millet Grain Salad, 51
Nopales Salad (cactus salad), Theresa's, 60
Orzo Primavera Salad, 48
Pasta Salad with Peanut Dressing, 50
Potato Salad, Dawn's Famous, 44
Spinach-Pine Nut Salad, 45
Summer Pasta Salad with Grilled Vegetables, 42
Tabbouleh, 55
Yum Yum Salad, Roxanne's Favorite, 43

Main Dishes
African Stew, 128
Aromatic Vegetables, 149
Asian Soy "Chicken" Rolls, 134-135
Asparagus Stir Fry, 104
Barley-Zucchini Sauté, 82
BBQ Vegetables, 144
Black-Eyed Peas and Rice, 153
Broccoli Casserole, 101
Bulgur with Cabbage and Three Onions, 125
Butternut Stew with Tofu and Pine Nuts, 158
Cabbage and Walnut Stir-Fry, 94
Calabacitas, 67
Carrot Casserole, 139
Carrot Couscous with Chickpeas, 131
Cauliflower Casserole, 100
Cheesy, Zucchini Rice Bake, 102
Chilaquileas with Beans, 130-131
Chunky Vegetable Paella, 108
Confetti Rice, 155
Curried Barley with Portobello Mushrooms, 65
Curried Parsnip Pie, 110-111
Curry Casserole, 136
Eggplant Boats, 115
Eggplant Parmesan, 72
Eggplant-Polenta Casserole, 78

Vegetarian Delights

Eggplant Sandwiches with Pepper Yogurt Sauce, 86
Falafel, 105
Favorite Spinach with Filo, 107
Fideo, Family Favorite, 90
Fiesta Tamale Pie, 88
Flavorful Vegetarian Stew, 121
Flemish Style Red Cabbage, 127
Fried Scrambled Tofu (eggs), 76
Greek Potato Casserole, 138
Heavenly Shepherd Pie, 93-94
Hominy Stew, 142
Hot Nut Loaf, 124
Indian Spiced Cauliflower, 146
Leek Quiche, 63
Lumpia, 147
Magnificent Zucchini, 106
Mexican Delight, 77
Mousakka, 116-117
Pasta and Mushroom Casserole, 114-115
Peanut and Potato Loaf, 123
Pepper and Potato Tortilla (from Spain), 99
Pita Pizzas, 98
Portobello Pizzettas, 91
Potato Almond Loaf, 151
Potato and Cabbage Croquettes, 96
Potato and Caramelized Onion Tart, 66
Potato and Parsnip Delish, 113
Potato-Spinach Bake, 64
Potatoes with Blue Cheese and Walnuts, 104-105
Quinoa with Radishes, 137
Red Cabbage with Millet, 141
Sautéed Spinach with Garlic, 150
Scalloped Potatoes, 154
Sesame Tofu with Vegetable Rice, 81
Sloppy Joes, 135-136
Spelt Patties with Cheese Sauce, 140
Spicy Black-Eyed Peas, 157
Spinach Stuffed Pasta Shells, 74
Squash with Peanuts, 122
Stuffed Bell Peppers, Millan's Mother's Famous, 89
Stuffed Cabbage Rolls, Jeff's Favorite, 112
Stuffed Egg Plant, 95
Stuffed Potato and Parsnip, 111
Stuffed Rolled Eggplant, Delicious, 156
Stuffed Squash, 152
Stuffed Zucchini, Millan's Favorite, 143
Sweet Potato Casserole, 79
Tangy Fricassè, 109
Tempeh Triangles with Piccata Sauce, 133-134
Tempura Vegetables with Dipping Sauce, 148
Tofu and Vegetables, 97
Tomatoes Stuffed with Corn Soufflé, 145
Tortellini with Roasted Vegetable Sauce, 85
Tortilla Torte, 129
Vegetable Fiesta Casserole, 92
Vegetable Hearty Stew, 80
Vegetable Patties, 71
Vegetable Pie, 118
Vegetable Pie, Fresh, 84
Vegetable Pockets, 132
Vegetable Pot Pie, 75-76
Vegetable Stir Fry, Millan's, 68
Vegetarian Chili, 103
Vegetarian Enchiladas, Millan's, 69-70
Vegetable Lasagna, 73
Vegetarian Spaghetti, 120
Veggie Burrito, 126
White Bean Casserole, 87
Zucchini Pie, 83
Zucchini Stuffed with Soy Cream Cheese, 119

Desserts

Apple-Lemon Fritters, 169
Applesauce Soufflé, 174-175
Banana Bread, 173
Bread Pudding, Easy, 178
Bump and Crunch Cookies, 172
Carrot Cake, Healthy Tasty, 175-176
Coconut Macaroons, 161
Custard, Lareesa's Favorite, 167
Fruit and Nut Balls, 177
Gingerbread, 174
Golden Harvest Cake, 166-167
Hemp Seed Balls, 163
Hot Carob Delight, 180
Milkshake, Cream Banana Date, 164
Noodle Kugel, 165
Nut Milk, 180
Nutty Cookies, 178
Orange Honey Cake, 164
Peach Cobbler, Louise Edward's, 162
Peanut Butter Cookies, 176
Pineapple Upside Down Cake, 171
Pumpkin Rice Pudding, 177
Raw Apple Cake, 168
Sweet Potato Pie, My Dear Louise's, 170
Zucchini Crown Bread, 179